Through faith in Christ, we are not excused from the necessity of overcoming our mountains but rather we are expected to live and grow through them. God is present with His people to assist, strengthen, and encourage us, so that during your present struggle you might hear these words, "What have you already overcome that allows you to face this challenge?"
– Pastor Dave McCue, Colfax & St John United Methodist Churches

Every opposition in life is bound to test our faith in God. One thing is certain, those that trust in God will always overcome in the end. Looking down from the mountaintop, we appreciate how far we are removed from the valley.
– Pastor Muyiwa Karunwi, RCCG, Greener Pastures Assembly, New York

Francis Adewale is so full of love, joy and thankfulness that you can't be in his presence and not be affected. I am sure this book will touch the lives of all who read it.
– Pastor Nick Hasselstrom, His Banner Church, Moscow, Idaho

Pastor Francis is very knowledgeable in the Scriptures. He is a practical man with a teachable heart and gentle spirit. Based on his life experience as a legal practitioner, this book will touch and transform the lives of its readers, both believers and unbelievers.
– Pastor Samuel Olu Sorinmade – The Redeemed Christian Church of God, Cornerstone Worship Center for all Nations, Melrose, Massachusetts

The mountaintop is the promised land of every man. No man is born at the top to travel down; we all start out at the bottom and go up. Those who fail, talk more about life's obstacles, while successful people talk about possibilities, even in adverse circumstances. I recommend this book to all those on their way to the top.
– Pastor Bayo Fadugba, RCCG Dominion Chapel, Houston, Texas

Mountains come in various shapes and dimensions in one's life. The author leads the reader on a practical journey to understand mountains and the attitude of man towards them. If you are ready to move to the next level in any area of your life, then this is a must-read book.

– Muyiwa Oyekan, Associate Pastor, Kingdom Ambassadors Christian Center, Maryland

Life's mountains are surmountable through our strong faith in Christ. Pastor Francis shares his practical experience of overcoming challenges while climbing the ladder of life. I highly recommend this book, OVER THE MOUNTAINS, for spiritual edification and breakthrough in climbing your own mountains.

– Rev Ademoyegun A. Oyekan, District Overseer, Foursquare Gospel Church, Sagamu, Nigeria

Over The Mountains

Cultivating the Attitude Needed to
Surmount Life's Mountainous Challenges

Francis Adewale

*D*EDICATION

To my lovely wife,
Olamide Yetunde Adetoro Adewale,
you complete me.

To our adorable children,
Samuel, Deborah, David, Daniel & Sarah,
I love you all.

MY INSPIRATION
HABAKKUK'S PRAYER

This prayer was sung by the prophet Habakkuk:

I have heard all about you, Lord, and I am filled with awe by the amazing things you have done. In this time of our deep need, begin again to help us, as you did in years gone by. Show us your power to save us. And in your anger, remember your mercy. I see God, the Holy One, moving across the deserts from Edom and Mount Paran. Selah.

His brilliant splendor fills the heavens, and the earth is filled with his praise! What a wonderful God he is! Rays of brilliant light flash from his hands. He rejoices in his awesome power...

Even though the fig trees have no blossoms, and there are no grapes on the vine; Even though the olive crop fails, and the fields lie empty and barren; Even though the flocks die in the fields, and the cattle barns are empty, yet I will rejoice in the Lord!

I will be joyful in the God of my salvation! The Sovereign Lord is my strength! He will make me as surefooted as a deer, and brings me safely over the mountains.

(Habakkuk 3:1-4, 17-19)(NLT) [1]

CONTENTS

FOREWORD

When Francis Adewale first arrived in Spokane, God showed us that he was 'key' to our ministry, valuable and precious to the Lord. God's word has been fulfilled as Pastor Francis has become an integral part of Spokane Dream Center as an Associate Pastor and Director of our Bible School. Our church has been enriched by his powerful teachings and godly example of walking in honor and integrity.

Over the Mountains laced with profound, practical examples embraces the challenge of overcoming mountains. Mountains are a daily part of our lives. God wants to produce in each one of us, not only mountain-moving faith, but mountain-climbing faith. This book will encourage you to take hold of this overcoming faith. It is God's desire for you. In so doing, you will draw closer to Him and conquer the mountains in your life. With God all things are possible.

–Pastors Dave and Alice Darroch, Spokane Dream Center, Spokane Valley, WA

* * *

In the author's words, mountains represent seemingly big problems; hindrances to progress that keep many people from reaching their God-given dream. It's true that mountains are difficult to physically remove. However, on the authority of the word of God, they can be moved.

Mountains movers are ordinary men who align with this extraordinary God through understanding and using the authority vested in them by God to attain an extraordinary level of achievement. The author, out of his wealth of experience in the Lord, has written a powerful exposition on this important subject. I recommend it to believers of all races, denominations and ages.

–Pastor Patrick I. Mejeidu LL.B, B.L. Dip. Theo. Secretary, Board of Coordinators, Redeemed Christian Church of God, North America Headquarters, Greenville, TX

Your attitude determines your altitude.

PREFACE
THE DOORWAY TO THE MOUNTAIN

There is a mountain in the distant West
That, sun-defying, in its deep ravines
Displays a cross of snow upon its side.
–Henry Wadsworth Longfellow[1]

Life is like a mountain. Masses of people are at the bottom, but the few who distinguish themselves are at the top. Most people turn away from facing the mountain's challenge, while a few bold ones run to the peak at great expense. The outstanding few who will stand at the summit will endure hardship, forsake many of life's pleasures and summon something deep within themselves, higher than the mountain before them, to enable them to reach the zenith.

I wrote the above paragraph on a doodle note on my iPad long before the thought of writing this book crossed my mind. That changed on a dark winter day, late one Friday afternoon, when one of the support staff at the public law firm where I work noticed me lugging around tomes of books on rock climbing. She tapped me on the shoulder and inquired about what I intended to do with all the books on a subject I had previously shown no interest.

I was a tad nonplussed. Looking up, I explained to her, "Each time I look back at my life I feel like someone climbing an insurmountable mountain."

She gave me a blank look and then turned around and walked away. The gentle tapping sound of her stiletto heels on the carpet echoed through the office as she approached her cubicle.

A few hours later, she returned. Quietly, she asked, "Are you serious about what you said earlier?"

"Yes," I replied. "Why did you walk away without letting me explain what I meant?"

"Honestly, I thought you overheard me talking about my own life." She went on to say that she always felt like her life had been a series of difficult, insurmountable challenges with little or no training or skill about how to navigate its many contours and jagged edges. Immediately, I sat up at my desk giving her my full attention.

My initial thought in writing this book was to reflect on my own personal experiences and challenges while climbing life's many "Rocky Mountains" and navigating through troublesome times. The thought of someone else having the same experience immediately peaked my interest and confirmed to me that this was indeed a book I needed to write.

My research involved studying mountains, hills and rocks in history and the Bible in addition to learning about the many courageous people who dared to climb them.

This book explores both my challenges and experiences and the reflections of others in navigating life's mountainous travails against the backdrop of my studies of the Bible and history. My hope is that you will find a few nuggets of truth to lighten your own load on this journey we call life.

There are many who believe that no personal experience is necessarily replicable and that each and every one of us has to experience life's challenges in our own unique way.

John Muir, the Scottish-born American author of a widely read book on adventures in the Sierra Nevada mountains of California, was once quoted as saying, "I have a low opinion of books; they are but piles of stones set up to show coming travelers where other minds have been, or at best, signal smokes to call attention. No amount of word-making will ever make a single soul to *know* these mountains. As well seek to warm the naked and frost-bitten by lectures on caloric and pictures of flame. One day's exposure to mountains is better than cartloads of books…All that is required is exposure, and purity of material "The pure in heart shall see God!" No synonym for God is so perfect as Beauty. Whether as seen carving the lines of the mountains with glaciers or gathering matter into stars, or planning the movements of water, or gardening – still all is Beauty."[2]

> **There is no doubt that man's greatest ignorance is lack of knowledge about his own source and potential.**

I am, however, convinced that while this may be true of the topography of mountains, it may not necessarily apply to all metaphorical mountains nor to all mountaineers. More often than not, we still learn from each other because we are all pilgrims of the vertical. And if the journey is vertical, we are bound to run into each other on our way up the mountain. Even Muir agreed that mountainous experiences move men and bring advancements to civilization. He said, "The mountains are fountains of men as well as of rivers, of glaciers, of fertile soil. The great poets, philosophers, prophets, able men whose thoughts and deeds have moved the world, have come down from the mountains – mountain-dwellers who have grown strong there with the forest trees in Nature's work-shops."[3] The mistake some romantic environmentalists make is to equate beauty in created things with the majesty of the Creator; forgetting the fact that the Creator brings beauty out of ashes.

More importantly, a vertical journey compels travelers to look up and every attempt to look up will draw us to the One who is above. After all, as the Bible says, "He who comes from above is above all; He who is of the earth is earthly and speaks of the earth. He who comes from heaven is above all." (John 3:31) Likewise, when we look up, we tend to see the footprints of those who have gone before us. The tortuous path they took, the pain they endured, the joy and the triumph they celebrated at the peak often calls us to dare to do the same.

I owe much of the inspiration for writing this book as well as a good amount of the textual context to two powerful men of God whose sermons, books and lectures motivated me to get up from my couch, live the word and overcome! Pastor Enoch Adejare Adeboye's many sermons on the process of mountain climbing and Bishop Mensah Otabil's sermon on mountain-moving faith stick out above all the other books and sermons that have guided my journey on the mountain of life.

The two messages may seem irreconcilable to many, but by the help of the Holy Spirit, I not only understood them to be two sides of the same coin, I also found the grace to live by their tenets. Consequently, I owe much of the theological underpinnings of this book (albeit the part that is good) to these two illustrious sons of Africa, while the many errors you may find are totally mine. Many of my own sermons and testimonies are included to highlight the biblical admonition that the letter kills but the Spirit gives life!

Our task is not necessarily to understand the many contours and jagged edges of the mountains we face but to conquer them and emerge victorious in our life's journey. Knowledge and its right application is a powerful tool in driving away fear, ignorance and failure.

As Don Mellor was famously quoted to have said in, "Pilgrims of the Vertical", each mountain sojourner and traveler often "read the same news and editorials, climbers across the country share the same information, if not the same values."[4] In fact, as we often hear people say "experience is learning from our mistakes and wisdom is learning from the mistakes of others as we all stand on the shoulders of those who have gone before us."

I have been privileged for more than 10 years to teach a three-hour Friday class for Spokane Dream Center's Men's and Women's Discipleship Programs. During that time, I have seen men and women whose lives were nearly ruined by life's problems such as drug and alcohol addiction and many other life-controlling problems, turn around and start to dream again. For many of those who break through, it is largely due to the encouragement, instruction and good counsel they receive as well as the grace of the Almighty. I have seen men from all walks of life overcome broken hearts and shattered lives and then climb heights they had never dreamed of, surmounting many travails and pains as they arrive at the summit of their life dreams.

Many give up on life's challenges, often, because they look at them as insurmountable. Some give up looking for the compass they need to navigate life. Some make it to the bottom of the mountain, raise up their heads to look at the top and then throw up their hands dejectedly walking away with sullen faces; choosing to dwell in the lowlands rather than face life's difficult challenges. Some even summon enough courage to ascend the mountain and midway tumble down, crashing back to earth as soon as they suffer a bit of a setback.

I write not as someone who has attained or reached the pinnacle of my own mountainous challenges but as someone who is determined to continue the journey to the zenith using the experience, skills and discoveries I've learned on my journey.

I am convinced I am not alone in this quest. Many will come away from this book delighted to find the right mental attitude to surmount their challenges, while others will find the content confirms what they already know. Others will dismiss its wisdom because they're not ready to conquer the mountain. Whatever your take on the book, my plea is that you will prepare yourself for the challenges of life. Because when the storms of life rage, it is what you know, believe and act upon that will make the difference between life and death. Mark Obmascik tells of a father and daughter who pushed on to the summit of Quandary Peak, one of the Fourteeners in Colorado in the United States of America. They pushed on despite an approaching thunderstorm; their lightning-scarred bodies were found the next day. He also tells the story of a twenty-five year old skier who set off alone into the back country without telling anyone where he was headed; "four days later, on Christmas Day, his leg was found sticking out of the bottom of an 1,800 foot avalanche chute on the Quandary Peak."[5] In all of these instances, a cursory look at the weather report or information would have made a difference. You have to open your ears to information and act on it.

Generally, my approach is to look at life's mountainous challenges from the totality of my limited, but yet rich worldview, personal revelation, and my relationship with others combined with my experience as an African, albeit a naturalized United States of America citizen. No human being can lay claim to a magic formula that cures all of man's life challenges and I do not posit to have all the answers. What I do know is my own experience in the quest for these answers.

My search for answers has inevitably led me to the Source and Creator of all things, the one who spoke all the rocks and mountains into existence through the power of His Word. If this revelation will dissuade you from continuing to read this book, I urge you to hear me out. Even though I offer no apologies for my conviction, this one thing I urge and plead for, consider my message before you dismiss the messenger.

There is no doubt that man's greatest ignorance is lack of knowledge about his own source and potential. When we discover our source, we will surely be on our way to fulfill our potential. Our Source will direct us to the instruction manual He has prescribed for us. I am convinced that some of the unique attitudes or qualities required of a good rock or mountain climber are uniquely relevant to our life challenges. Attitudes such as vision and passion enhanced by initiative and teamwork built with the strong tools of innovation and persistence, then groomed by discipline and focus coupled with patience and compassion will be explored in this book so that we can all discover how to cultivate them in our own lives.

This book is dedicated to helping millions of people who are stuck at the foot of the mountain when the peak beckons them. It will help you discover once again your true potential and equip you with the right mental attitude to start ascending to the heights you thought were beyond your reach. As I stated earlier, wisdom is learning from other people's mistakes and challenges. So get ready to learn from my experiences and those who have traversed the mountains before us.

Over The Mountains

Prologue
Escape to the Mountains

*So it came to pass, when they had brought them outside, that he said,
"Escape for your life! Do not look behind you nor stay anywhere
in the plain. Escape to the mountains, lest you be destroyed.*
– Genesis 19:17

The carnal man will almost always choose the easy, less arduous route to life. The story of Lot in the first book of the Bible is symptomatic of man's desire to always choose the physical to the detriment of his own spiritual well-being. In the quest to please our fleshly desire, we will often ignore spiritual direction, disrespect spiritual authority and even go as far as mortgaging our future in order to secure temporal enjoyment.

There are so many disturbing patterns in Lot's life we can learn from starting from the moment his uncle, Abraham, brought him out of Ur of Chaldea to Canaan, the Promised Land. It is evident that Lot was blessed because of his association with Abraham. They both became so blessed and "their possessions were so great that they could not dwell together." (Genesis 13:6b) As a result of their wealth, their herdsmen began to clash, and Lot being the junior one, did not deem it fit to squelch the dispute caused by the servants. He chose to ignore and pretend he did not see the fracas. Again, Abraham had to point it out and request separation.

When Abraham asked Lot to choose which land he would prefer, one would have thought Lot would defer to the elderly Abraham and simply say "you first". But the Bible says, "And Lot lifted his eyes and saw all the plain of Jordan, that it was well watered everywhere (before the Lord destroyed Sodom and Gomorrah) like the garden of the Lord, like the land of Egypt as you go toward Zoar. Then Lot chose for himself all the plain of Jordan, and Lot journeyed east. And they separated from each other." (Genesis 13:10-11)

Sometimes separation can be difficult but it has to be done. We need to remember that when God called Abraham to leave Ur of Chaldea, He never asked him to take Lot with him. In fact, the Lord said, "Get out of your country, from your family and from your father's house." (Genesis 12:1)

In my own experience, I have seen many enter our discipleship program after a life of drug and alcohol addiction who cannot let go of past destructive relationships that used to fuel their binge drinking or drug use. These are people called to separate themselves and come and learn at the feet of Jesus for one year but they cannot bear to leave their "house or brothers or sisters or father or mother or wife or children or lands", for Christ and the gospel's sake." (Mark 10:29b)

Some would obey the call to separate themselves to the Lord and then bring something or someone from their past with them. This is where Abraham was when God called him out of Ur of Chaldea. We have to learn to obey God's specific instructions and divine direction for our lives.

The decision to bring Lot with him had ramifications beyond their years together. The escalation of the conflict between Abraham's and Lot's servants would not have happened had Abraham obeyed God completely. The steadfast love of the Lord never ceases and He is always there for us when we realize the error of our ways and make amends. Abraham immediately realized the need for separation and invited Lot to choose.

When making his choice, Lot chose based on the flesh and so he chose the plains where the land was easier, so he wouldn't need to climb the mountain. The Bible says, "Abram dwelt in the land of Canaan, and Lot dwelt in the cities of the plain and pitched his tent even as far as Sodom." (Genesis 13:12) Notice here that Lot even though he chose the plain, was not at this time dwelling in Sodom, he merely "pitched his tent even as far as Sodom." You see, "a little leaven leavens the whole lump." (I Corinthians 5:6b)

The Bible says flee all appearance of evil. Many people when they are under the grace of Christ often play with little compromises. They comfort themselves with the fact that they have not gone too far. It is only a little. Forgetting that a little compromise here and there will often lead to a big backsliding! We have seen people bring all kinds of materials and objects to the discipleship program. Some will come to the program with inappropriate pictures of their girlfriend stuffed under their pillow. Others arrive with their bong believing it is too expensive to throw away. The problem with all of this is that they may not be in Sodom but they have carelessly pitched their tent near Sodom as these foreign objects often directly link them to the past they need to leave behind.

You can almost predict what will happen next as compromise continues to erode Lot's already shaky foundation. By the time we reach Genesis 14:12, we find that Lot is already a resident of Sodom. In my experience teaching at our discipleship house, I have discovered that many of those who speak fondly of their past and hold on to those memories including tokens of their past never finish the program. They often leave before completing the full year and those who stick it out until the end of the first year quickly relapse.

At the Dream Center, we often have to come in like Abraham and rescue "lots" of our disciples. Their situation is similar to Lot's. Even when he saw people from Sodom and Gomorrah fleeing to the mountains to escape the destruction in the city (Genesis 14:10), Lot returned to Sodom to dwell at the gate. (Genesis 19:1) Our disciples often return to their own gates, the sin and addiction, that initially brought them to us.

We have to remember that Lot himself was at all times a righteous person as II Peter 2:7-8 clearly reminds us, his problem was a little compromise here and there, particularly his desire not to heed the commandment of the Lord to escape to the mountain. At one point, he even called the people of Sodom, his brethren, (Genesis 19:7) thinking they had accepted him as one of their own, but they still referred to him as a sojourner who was trying to judge them.

A little while ago, one of our disciples approached the pastor and said that he no longer wanted to live a "religious life" and was willing to entertain "a little wine here and there" even though he was just coming out of a serious alcohol addiction. Not long after that, he graduated to smoking marijuana and other dangerous drugs. In the end, he nearly lost his mind.

We always make excuses for our sins even knowing that God frowns on sin. We deflect our shame by finding fault in those whose lives convict us of sin by accusing them of controlling us and robbing us of our freedom. Creating a diversion, we try and put the blame on others rather than owning up to our own inadequacies and repenting.

Most of us are not willing to push ourselves too hard, so we settle for less. We choose a nearby city instead of the city on the mountain appointed for us by the Lord.

Avoiding sin is not being religious; it is a commandment of the Lord. He said we should flee all appearances of evil. (I Thessalonians 5:22) Under the guise of saving the world, many Christians choose to live a worldly lifestyle evidenced by a life of compromise. They believe that by taking on the mantle of the world they can bring people to Christ, forgetting that compromising with the world is not what leads people to salvation; it is only by the blood of Jesus. The shocking fact that Lot would even contemplate offering his virgin daughters to the vicious mob to do what they wanted with them, in lieu of the two messengers of the Lord, clearly shows the extent to which his morality had been severely lowered by Sodom's standards.

More shocking is his desire to choose to escape to a little city near Sodom instead of fleeing to the mountains, as the two angels suggested. Even as the two angels were pulling him "kicking and screaming" out of Sodom, Lot convinced them to allow him to settle in a small city near Sodom. His aversion to climbing the mountain of morality and fleeing instead to the plains of compromise cost him all his possessions and members of his family. He pleaded, "Indeed now, your servant has found favor in your sight, and you have increased your mercy which you have shown me by saving my life; but I cannot escape to the mountains, lest some evil overtake me and I die. See now, this city is near enough to flee to, and it is a little one; please let me escape there (is it not a little one?) and my soul shall live." (Genesis 19:19-20) [emphasis added]

When we warn the graduates of our Men's and Women's Discipleship programs about the dangers of compromise, they think we are trying to control them. As I write this book, one of the men at our church's discipleship house came to me seeking my guidance. He was wondering if he should leave the program. I immediately directed him to Genesis 19 and told him that God is often calling us to escape to the mountain because the mountain represents a place where Christians are supposed to gather together in unity. (Psalm 133) When brethren dwell together in unity, the anointing flows over them, and there, the Lord commands a blessing.

A mountain is a place where we gather together to spread the gospel of Christ. Isaiah 52:7 says, "How beautiful upon the mountains are the feet of him who brings good news, who proclaims peace, who brings glad tidings of good things, who proclaims salvation, who says to Zion, "Your God reigns!" It is also a place of deliverance and holiness. Obadiah 1:17 says, "But on Mount Zion there shall be deliverance, and there shall be holiness; the house of Jacob shall possess their possessions." The church is our Mount Zion. I often laugh when people say they are hurting or sick and choose not to come to church. Church is the first place we should run when we are sick, tired, depressed or facing life's challenges.

The reason we stay away from church is likely because of our own little compromises rather than anything else. Some say, "I don't want people to judge me", forgetting it is the Holy Spirit through the Word of God that judges us. One of our brothers took me to his new house upon his graduation from the discipleship program. I tried to open his refrigerator and he wouldn't let me. He didn't want me to see the wine, beer and whatever else was in there. I tried to look at the history tab on the browser of his computer and he wouldn't let me. Needless to say, he was back in the discipleship house within months after my visit. He said, "The world is a jungle out there." I told him his compromise feeds the jackals and the hyenas in the jungle.

What was responsible for Lot's aversion to escape to the mountain, as directed by the two angels, and why did he choose to live in the plains? It was a direct command coupled with several pleadings by the two angels, and yet, Lot voluntarily chose a nearby city. Do you actually think he believed what he said about being killed in the mountains? Men will always justify their decision to disobey the commandment of the Lord. The clue to understanding Lot's choice is right there in Genesis 19:16, the Bible said "he lingered". He lingered because of the lures and cares of the plains. We are too often satisfied with a life of mediocrity. Matthew Henry put it succinctly when he wrote:

> It was Lot's weakness to think a city of his own choosing safer than the mountain of God's appointing. And he argued against himself when he pleaded, *Thou hast magnified thy mercy in saving my life, and I cannot escape to the mountain*; for could not he that plucked him out of Sodom, when he lingered, carry him safely to the mountain, though he began to tire? Could not he that saved him from greater evils save him from the less?

He insists much in his petition upon the smallness of the place: *It is a little one, it is not?* Therefore, it was to be hoped, not so bad as the rest. [1]

To fulfill our potential, we may have to go to the mountain chosen for us by the Lord. We know God expects our very best as we climb this mountain. However, most of us are not willing to push ourselves too hard, so we settle for less. We choose a nearby city instead of the city on the mountain appointed for us by the Lord. Lot lingered because too much of his heart was in Sodom.

As David Guzik rightfully argued, the "lack of urgency to obey God (even when it is necessary and good for you) is a common sign of compromise and a backslidden condition." [2] His "Please, no, my Lord" rings in our ears today as we struggle with our own obedience to the commandments of the Lord. One thing we find in the midst of the destruction of the inhabitants of the plain is that God will always answer the prayers of intercessors. He saved Lot's life because of Abraham's intercessory prayers. (Genesis 19:29) Lot's choice of the plains over the mountain had drastic consequences including the loss of all his possessions and his wife was turned into a pillar of salt. A choice between the spiritual and the physical almost always has consequences. As Christ himself said, "Remember Lot's wife." (Luke 17:32)

A divine call to escape to the mountain may not necessarily be settling for a less taxing place; it may also be a divine call to step up and fulfill our potential. Some are punching below their weight and ready to settle for less even though God has a greater calling for them. I know that because I was once there myself. This is why the mountain metaphor is very apposite.

I remember exactly the moment when I got the final results of my Elementary School Third Grade Exams, which we call, Primary School Class Three Examinations Report Card in Nigeria. It still remains vividly etched in my memory as I write this. First of all, the report card contained more red ink than blue ink. I had failed every subject I sat for that year. The teacher, for a reason best known to her, decided to write in all caps in the comment section: "ALABA ADEWALE IS BEING PROMOTED ON TRIAL BECAUSE I BELIEVE HE COULD DO BETTER THAN THIS RESULT SHOWS."

I still don't know why he promoted me on trial despite failing every subject. I was 47th in an exam conducted for 49 pupils in my class. I was hopeless, that was what my dad told me the previous year when I was last in my class. I failed every subject then, too. In fact, I had failed every grade since I started my elementary education. I could not pass any measure or test of intelligence I was examined on, including the study of the Yoruba language, my mother tongue!

The teacher had written in the subject column, "oburu ja i!" which literarily translated means "despicable result and grade!" I didn't want to go home, so I avoided my siblings as much as possible by loitering around the school until everyone left and the school principal was about to lock the gate. He noticed me sitting by the school's perimeter fence and summoned me to come to him by nodding in my direction.

"Hey, you, what are you doing sitting there, aren't you going home?"

He looked at my sullen, contorted face noticing the sadness and took pity on me. Not bothering to wait for my response, he curtly answered his own question.

"You failed, right?"

I could not get myself to respond in words, so I nodded my head up and down. Picking up my report card, he smiled mischievously. He took one hard look at it and said, "At least you are going to the next class, so cheer up and go home to your parents. Tomorrow, I will talk to your teacher and find out why he promoted a student that failed in all subjects."

> *In the quest to please our fleshly desire, we often ignore spiritual direction, disrespect spiritual authority and even go as far as mortgaging our future at the price of filthy lucre in order to secure temporal enjoyment.*

His words sent shivers down my spine and felt like a dagger in my heart. I thought I had gotten my gracious teacher in trouble. I said to myself, "Now the poor teacher has to defend my "on trial status" due to my cowardly refusal to go home when school was over."

Finally, the school principal asked me if I wanted him to escort me home. Sensing the implication, I politely declined. I picked myself up and started walking home very slowly, contemplating the painful fate that awaited me.

On my way home, I had to cross two or three major arterial intersections, and on each of them, I hoped that a big truck would drive by and run me over. I also had to cross the Oora River by our house. Here again, I wished the river would sweep me away but I made it to the other side without any problem.

The echoes of my father's numerous warnings to me the previous year kept ringing in my ears. I recalled him yelling with great emphasis, "I can no longer tolerate your penchant for wasting my hard-earned money; you are as useless as your mother. I paid school fees for you to excel. The kids that passed had only one head and one brain like you. You have no excuse for poor grades."

Remember, before this, I had failed every final exam I ever sat for and on each of those occasions my Dad said he was done with me.

My father's house is located on a hilltop at the outskirts of my hometown called Ilesha, Osun State, Nigeria. As I made my way up the hill, I tried to imagine what fate awaited me. I knew I wouldn't be treated with kid gloves. I had failed again when every other kid in my dad's house had passed.

As I ruminated over my fate, with a forlorn look and sad face, I plodded home slowly. I kept thinking of the inevitable "beat down" I was going to receive from my father. I had no other place to go. I was between a rock and a hard place and nothing was going to spare me from the horse tail whip he always had ready for days like today.

Finally, I reached the house and could see the whip waiting for me. My siblings had obviously "told on me" before I got home. My father did not allow me to say the customary Yoruba welcome greeting before he picked up the whip and got into action. I went down on my knees and took the punishment.

As the beating and whipping continued, he kept asking me why I failed and expected me to answer as he mercilessly beat me. The more I tried to proffer an incomprehensible answer, the faster the whip went up and down lacerating my back, burning and burrowing into my dark skin. In between the whippings, I glanced at my body and could see my skin was fused to my uniform with my own blood serving as the elastic glue keeping the two together.

When my father finally relented, I stood up and ran for my life although I had no idea where to go. I just wanted to run as far away from home as possible, from my father, the punishment, and most importantly, the searing pain from the whip's stinging lashes. By now the street was dark and desolate, which is common with tropical Africa. The night was alive with a symphony of sound from frogs, critters and fireflies that accompanied me as I kept running.

Weary from the beating and my run, I arrived at my mother's house near the outer edge of town. From her balcony, she saw my approach and immediately ran out to me. Peeling off the remnants of my blood-soaked clothes, she then guided me to a hot bath. This didn't mean my mother condoned my failure, because while tending to my poor physical state she kept remonstrating me for my shortfall. Sternly, she said, "Forget about any holidays this year." Her punishment for me was to stay at home, and on no account, could I go play soccer with the other boys on our street.

True to her word, everyone that came to visit us during the vacation holiday would be reminded by my mother of my utter failure in school. Some of them often had advice for me. Some would say, "You ought to read more", "You should study more" or "You should pay more attention in class." Others would encourage me to "just do what the teacher requires of you." It was as if the answer to my problem was as simple as that, "just do it!"

As young as I was, I remember thinking to myself, "I have tried all of these and none of it works for me." I was never a truant in school. I rarely arrived late and I was always obedient in class. It was not that I did not try to read, when I wasn't playing street soccer. And the reason I had to mix soccer with reading was because I rarely understood what I was reading, so I gave up in frustration. I didn't understand mathematics or science.

The other problem was that I could barely remember what the teachers said within a few minutes after class was out and I definitely couldn't recall it the next day. On every test, I could neither understand the question nor follow the instructions preceding the question, because I couldn't read or understand any of it.

My mother tried to pay the class teacher, who had a private tutoring class at her home, to help me but the results weren't any different. The teacher gave up and advised my mother to stop wasting her money. She told my mother, "Some people are meant for greatness while others are meant to serve great people. Your son is definitely not meant for anything great in life. He has a lot to learn and unfortunately time and tide wait for none. I am afraid life has passed him by." My mother nodded her head in agreement.

Following my teacher's devastating announcement, my mother discussed the possibility of withdrawing me from school and enrolling me as a bricklayer (masonry) with my uncle. She had no choice given the fact that my father insisted that he would no longer tolerate my spate of failures.

During that long vacation, my mother woke me up early every morning to go to my uncle's house on Imo Street; it was quite a long journey. Initially, I hated it and would grumble about walking the long distance. My mother insisted that I was to stay there until she got back from work. This achieved two purposes for her. On one hand, my uncle would at least ensure that I did something while my mother was away. On the other hand, it assured her that I wouldn't be playing soccer while she was at work.

My uncle was a book publishing agent as well as a bookseller, which meant that he had lots of books at his house. He would assign me books to read every day. Initially, since I could not read, he gave me a dictionary and started telling me the story from the books in such a way as to garner my interest until I started to read on my own. Then he introduced me to non-fiction books, and then fiction, and finally, textbooks.

At the end of each book, we would discuss what I learned. He would then tell me the personal history of the author and how they came to the publishing company without much money before they got published. He took my mind completely off my bad grades. When I returned home in the evening under the tropical setting sun, I would play indoor games like "ayo" with some of my "street" friends who came by when my mother had not yet returned from her shop.

One evening, one of them invited me to attend his grandmother's church. I asked him to tell his grandmother to specifically request permission from my mother. He did and when his grandmother came to our house, my mother, to my utter surprise, agreed that I should spend my evenings at the church.

It also happened that same year, the church choir director had a bitter disagreement with the other ministers and decided to leave the church, thus leaving the church's ongoing anniversary and annual Christmas drama planning and preparation in jeopardy.

The church hastily recruited a replacement choir director who, however, could not find enough cast members, as most of them left following the schism. So he turned to folks like me, who did not necessarily attend the church. He begged me to get involved and I reluctantly agreed to participate. The practice was grueling but I loved it. Again, it piqued my interest as it took my mind away from my poor school grades.

Within ten weeks, the Jesus passion play was ready and I was to be Peter. We put on a good show and quite a lot of people attended the premiere. It was such a success that everyone in my hometown was surprised. At the end of the drama, one of the church's assistant pastors who had seen my performance, approached and asked me to please come and visit his home as he had a gift for me as a reward for my performance.

At first, I didn't want to go, as I doubted his ability to buy a gift of any appreciative value on his meager income. It was well known that he was one of the poorest pastors in that church. Reluctantly, I decided to go visit him. When I arrived, the pastor was sitting in front of a one bedroom ramshackle house. He thanked me for coming and said, "I'm amazed at how quickly you picked up your lines and delivered them so distinctly. Surely many souls were won to the kingdom as a result of the drama." He then asked, "Is there anything in particular that you want the Lord to do for you?"

There is some anointing oil that will not flow until it is propelled by your determination and faith to reach the zenith of your problematic mountains.

I looked at him morosely, and just blurted out something along the lines of, "Well, if God wants to help, He should start by making me a brilliant student so I could start passing my exams." To this day, I cannot fathom where that came from.

But he heard me and again said, "Is that all you want?"

I mumbled something unintelligible that ended with the word, "yes."

Then he went inside, and it was a long time before he reappeared still muttering a prayer under his breath. As I looked up at him, I could read his lips repeating these words intermittently, "Every mountain of failure, I command you to move in the life of Alaba, in Jesus' name."

Apostolic Faith churches in Nigeria are well-known for their repetitive prayers, so I was not in any way surprised.

Later, he asked me to kneel down as he wanted to pray for me again. This time he said specifically while laying hands on me: "I say to you mountains of impossibility in the life of Alaba Adewale, I command you to move in Jesus' name." He kept repeating this prayer in one form or another for several minutes until he sensed a release in his spirit, then he started thanking, praising and worshipping God.

A little while later, he started thanking God again for all the souls reached through my ministration during the drama. He prayed that they would abide. He sang songs, prayed and worshiped God some more. It was as if he was having a mini-service in his small living room.

After what seemed to be an eternity, he stopped praying and asked me to stand up and go. "Make sure you read well before every exam." Before I left, he said, "I have nothing except a boiled egg." He prayed over the boiled egg and handed it to me, "Please enjoy it."

I left his house confused, angry and underwhelmed. Nevertheless, I ate the egg, as I was hungry and famished from all the prayer and the kneeling. I tried as much as possible to forget about this strange assistant pastor and his gift for me. When I got home, everyone was expecting me to bring at least a toy or gift home and they were all sorely disappointed when I told them my present was a mountain-moving prayer.

It was not until recently when I sat down to write this book that it dawned on me that since that fateful day, I have never failed another exam. The following year, even though I was promoted on trial, I was third in my class. By the time I finished high school, I had the best results in the whole school. My grades have never dipped below "B+" since that day. God indeed answered the prayer of a poor assistant pastor who had nothing but a boiled egg to give as a reward for a good performance to a guy coerced at the eleventh hour to play Peter in a small church anniversary/Christmas drama. The strangest thing about this experience is that the assistant pastor left the church before the end of that year and I never saw him again.

My mountain of failure was surmounted by a willingness to give my talents to God, which in turn made a poor assistant pastor pray to move the mountain of failure out of my life. Little did I know that as I spent my long vacation climbing the mountain of hardship by denying myself the joy of watching and playing soccer but choosing rather to serve in church where my talent was needed, God was preparing a poor assistant pastor to pray and move the mountain of failure in my life.

At this particular time, I was not born again or overly spiritual. I just needed to change my hopeless situation. I have found that people struggling through seemingly hopeless situations and circumstances don't care at all about philosophy, theology or psychology. Most people battling mountainous obstacles and challenges have probably heard and tried all of that and failed. What most people want is the reality of God's awesome presence. The price of life is Christ. Christ in us is the hope of glory. He already paid the price. God will always show up in a mysterious and powerful way. No wonder the Bible says, His ways are past finding out. (Romans 11:33)

I have gone to great lengths to retell this story to buttress the fact that sometimes in this life we go through things that are not necessarily meant to stop us but to promote us to a greater position. Some of the afflictions, problems and mountains we will face are not a satanic blockade but a divine arrangement to make us stronger and lead us to our destiny on higher ground.

I am not saying that God made me a dullard to teach me some profound lessons. What I am saying is that God allowed my afflictions to manifest His glorious presence in my life. As David rightly stated in the book of Psalms, "It is good for me that I have been afflicted, that I may learn your statutes." (Psalm 119:71) Before my divine encounter with this man of God, I never took God seriously. After that Christmas anniversary drama, I began to take my spiritual journey seriously. I started attending church and even joined my mother's local Catholic Church.

Some will read this story and point to the time I spent with my uncle learning how to read and take that as pivotal to my breakthrough. That would not be far from the truth, but previously when other family members had tried to teach me how to read and even my own class teacher made an effort, it never worked for me.

I am convinced that so many times God is waiting to turn our provocation to promotion if we let Him. Hannah needed a Peninnah (her rival) in her life to provoke her to pray an effectual fervent prayer without moving her lips before receiving her miracle. (I Samuel 1) God will often prepare us in a pressure cooker to manifest His glory in our life. Remember, you are the one that needs provokers, they don't need you. They are meant to open the door to your mountainous challenge. God will set you up for His glory.

There is some anointing oil that will not flow until it is propelled by your determination and faith to reach the zenith of your problematic mountains. When it is all over, your destiny will be manifested in your life. Since that dramatic failure in third grade, I completed a two-year graduate program in one year with the best results in the history of the program. I completed my law school program with great distinction, winning many laurels on the way.

God saw my perseverance and desire to change my fortune in life when He guided my steps to my uncle who encouraged me to read. He also guided my steps to participate in that small church anniversary drama and led a man of God to say to the mountain of impossibilities in my life to move. The same God that removed failure from my life is able to move every mountain of failure, lack, addiction and impossibility out of your life, in Jesus' name. You, too, can begin your journey with Christ today as you read this book.

PART I
UNDERSTANDING MOUNTAINS

*Mountain and rock climbing speak to the desire
of human beings to reach beyond our physical
and emotional limits, past morbid fear, fatigue and
excruciating pain to get to the apex of our dreams.*

CHAPTER ONE
MOUNTAINS EXPLAINED: PHYSICAL, METAPHYSICAL AND SPIRITUAL

I like the mountains, because they make me feel small…
They help me sort out what's important in life.
– Jeff Cruzan [1]

Some mountains have royalty written all over them, series of undulating spectacularly jagged mountains atop a gorgeous, lush plateau. They stare at you intently with a "bring it on" posture, defying anything around them to come and bow to their majesty. Admirers of these majestic peaks gape in awe of their grandiose cliffs while others choose to ignore them.

Great mountains with attitude often tower far and above their surroundings, be it cities, forests, rivers or canyons. They dominate the surrounding valley, topography and landscape with a dash of panache. Likely the summits of those rare huge mountains are close, tiny spaces where their shoulders like pyramids extend downward with couloirs all around their individually unique local reliefs. Passersby gape at them, tourists armed with cameras shoot away, and very few people who dare to ascend and descend these mountains understand the pain, hardship and difficulties they will endure along the way. Those who dare to defy the odds and reach the summit of their dream mountains will enjoy the expansive majestic view.

Other mountains may not necessarily be regal in their splendor. More often than not they are bland, uninteresting and dour in appearance. Some are barren and broad with large swaths of dismal jagged edges and forlorn peaks with screes and broken rock fragments. At the base, some have crags and valley shoulders rising petulantly along its talus and ridges. While some mountains rise from the valley with style and grace with endless varieties of flora and fauna nesting on its crevices and plateaus, others are uninhabitable, dripping with cold wintry snows or given to violent spasms of volcanoes erupting with regularity on conical hotspots, spewing lava and poisonous magmatic gases from a crater at its summit or from ugly viscous lava domes with slippery slopes.

In the end, all mountains, bland or regal, are crowns on the head of those who dare to reach their summits and come back to tell the tale of their ascent and descent. These heroes are the ones who make mountain climbing a worthwhile adventure. The metaphor of the regal and dour mountain is the story of man's quest to understand life as well as cultivate the earth's abundant resources for the benefit of mankind. The will to live in the midst of this dangerous, and yet beautiful world, is the saga of mountaineering.

An old mountaineering adage says, "In the mountains, no matter how tough you think you are, there is always someone tougher than you." Yet as difficult as these mountains are, they continue to lure modern-day dreamers, explorers, hobbyists and climbers. Dreamers are inspired to press on, while the indifferent recoil from them. Some mountains have inspired griots and kings, poets and artists, troubadours and soloists.

Mountain and rock climbing speak to the desire of human beings to reach beyond our physical and emotional limits, past morbid fear, fatigue and excruciating pain to get to the apex of our dreams. There is a reason why the two opposing armies were encamped on two adjacent mountains during one of the most important battles in the Bible between David and Goliath. (I Samuel 17:3)

If you linger at the top of one mountain, the world will move on while you celebrate yesterday's victories.

The lesson here is simple, both the Davids and Goliaths of this world will have to endure the excruciating hike up the mountain before the inevitable combat of destiny takes place. No matter the advantage you bring to the battle, be it height, strength, or dexterity in handling weapons, you must first get to the top of your mountain before you get the chance to show the world your skills. If Michael Jordan refused to show up for preseason conditioning training, there would have been no NBA finals nor six championship rings. He never would have been drafted to play in the NBA if he couldn't make his high school basketball roster.

More importantly, it is humbling to learn that as powerful as mountains are, they can be surmounted. I believe the purpose of mountains in our world is more spiritual than physical. But it is still important to note that these mountains exist because God put them there. It is our duty and responsibility to make sure that their beauty is not sacrificed because of our own selfish short-term interest. As Obsmascik noted, we can easily build another city, another bridge, even a bridge between mountains but the Rocky Mountains (to cite an example) were here before us. We need to appreciate the work of God even as we go beyond the physical to understand and overcome the mountainous problems in our lives.

Speaking of mountainous problems, we need to know that those who are not willing to go to the next level will die where they are. Sometimes the next level is beautiful but the process of getting there is arduous, painful and one long hard slog. It is only those who are willing to persevere and reach deep into the core of their being that will reach the peak of their careers and destiny.

Many things about the mountains ahead of you stare you down. Whatever the mountain may be, be it Mount Everest or Mount Kilimanjaro, a mountain of debt or a mountain of lack, a mountain of work or a mountain of adversity, a mountain of sickness or a mountain of affliction, whether they appear intimidating or overwhelming, you need to summon within you the deep riches of heaven to overcome it.

To have a mountaintop experience, you have to go over the mountain. In fact, the thought of failure is as intimidating as the effort you may need to be successful, so you should never let the enormity of the task deter you from your goals in life.

Mountains and mountain climbing can mean different things to different people. Some look at mountains and all they see are vertical heights and hard rough edges, while others look at mountains and see a durable, rich and beautiful abode, a hiding place or refuge. Many sports enthusiasts see mountains as a place to enjoy outdoor sports such as mountain climbing and hiking.

George Herbert Leigh Mallory, a famous British explorer and mountaineer, is famously quoted to have answered the question on why he wanted to climb Mount Everest by a curt reply, "Because it's there." His response has been called "the most famous three words in mountaineering." Life is about daring the impossible, the untested and doing it with panache. But it is not just daring for dare's sake. This is not a call to a life of risk-taking but a life of purpose.

Another British explorer and mountaineer, Sir Edmund Hillary, said, "If you climb a mountain for the first time and die on the descent, is it really a complete first ascent of the mountain? I am rather inclined to think personally that maybe it is quite important, the getting down, and the complete climb of a mountain is reaching the summit and getting safely to the bottom again." [2]

Many often make the mistake of likening life to the ascent of one solitary mountain. Forgetting that in the journey of life there are as many mountains to climb as there are rivers to cross. Thus conquering one mountain, very often, is preparation for the next one and the next one after that. Consequently, you have to put as much thought into the descent as you did the ascent.

If you linger at the top of one mountain, the world will move on while you celebrate yesterday's victories. The stories of Japanese holdouts–soldiers from World War II are apposite here. One such man is Hiroo Onoda, along with others that fought their way to possess an island in the Philippines during the war. Onoda along with three other fellow Japanese soldiers continued to occupy the mountains long after Japan had surrendered to the Allied Forces. They were on this mountain until 1974 when Onoda's former commander had to travel from Japan to personally issue orders relieving him of duty.

Onoda had spent almost 30 years holding out on the mountain long after the war, missing many of Japan's greatest accomplishments including the transition of Japanese society from an agrarian and traditionalist society to the technological giant and marvel we see today. He was fighting the local Philippines tribesmen dismissing every piece of information and pamphlet about Japan's defeat and surrender as propaganda.[3] These soldiers got carried away by their perceived victory in conquering one mountain forgetting that the war is a series of battles with many skirmishes and that holistic knowledge of the world is crucial to advancing to the next challenge in life.

Another misconception many make is to think that life begins and ends with daring to take a risk without purpose. Many people often take on an impossible task for the sake of fame, fortune and fun. Some get all they desire but still feel deeply the emptiness of life. They may get the fame, the money and lots of fun to boot and yet lose their family and everything they hold dear in the process. "Over the Mountains" is not a call for vain glory but a life of vision and purpose.

It is therefore important to make an attempt to define what we mean by 'mountain' so as to bring clarity and precision to our discussions on overcoming mountains throughout this book. Dictionary.com defines mountain as "a natural elevation of the earth's surface rising more or less abruptly to a summit, and attaining an altitude greater than that of a hill, usually greater than 2000 feet (610 meters)." In this book, we will use mountains and hills interchangeably, because what may appear to someone as a small hill problem may be a gargantuan Mount Kilimanjaro to others.

Additionally, Merriam Webster's Online Dictionary defines mountain as a "landform that rises well above its surroundings, generally exhibiting steep slopes, a relatively confined summit area, and considerable local relief (inequalities of elevation)."[4]

From these two definitions, we can deduce that mountains are generally bigger than any other thing around it. They are bigger than you and me. Mountains have steep slopes and considerable local relief. They have challenging cliff edges, steep slopes and difficult terrain. More importantly, every mountain has a relatively confined summit area where those who conquer it can stand and savor their victory. However, this is a natural or physical definition of a mountain and we shall seek to expand this definition beyond the physical.

Mountains are also used in our daily language and common idioms to reflect our common daily experiences. As Richard D. Patterson pointed out so eloquently, "one can have a "mountain of work" piled on his desk or face a "mountain of debt" or enjoy a "mountaintop experience." In sum, mountains and their significance enjoy wide familiarity in human experience." [5]

You may have been overwhelmed by the circumstances Patterson just spoke of, a mountain of work or a mountain of debt, but one thing you need to have confidence in, is the reality of God's abundant provision. Your "mountaintop experience" will be made much richer by the God who will give you wisdom that will help reduce your mountain of work and pay your mountain of debt.

The two common words used for mountain in the Bible are "*har*" in Hebrew and "*oros*" in Greek. The simple definition for each is mountain or hill, though they may indicate hill country or a mountainous region. [6] Many important events in the Bible that changed the course of history took place in and around mountain topography.

It is also important to note that a mountain can also be a metaphor or figurative expression for something different and difficult. So, metaphorically speaking, mountains could represent difficult challenges in our life or in the alternative, opportunities. They can be problems that are greater than all your money or influence or power can solve. They are physical challenges, health or marital, with difficult steep slopes, also disabilities, separation, divorce and the attendant pain and misery that necessarily follows.

Mountains, however, have something unique: a summit area. The summit area is often a relatively small area, and very few people make it there. Another definitive characteristic is that it has numerous local reliefs and contours where the less motivated often settle without getting to the summit. Many climbers start out with the hope of reaching the summit but end up wallowing in one of the mountain's many local reliefs, while their peers move on to the summit.

Both the Davids and Goliaths of this world will have to endure the excruciating hike up the mountain before the inevitable combat of destiny takes place.

According to these definitions, a mountain could be an obstruction to your destiny and the forward progress of your life or a hindrance to a life filled with joy, peace and tranquility. Mountains may appear as stubborn, stationary, even permanent situations in your life. Such situations could be relational (an issue between you and your boss), financial (a long owed debt or mortgage due), health challenges (sickness, affliction, diseases: terminal or short-term). Whatever it may be, it will often appear to you as an intimidating difficult circumstance. Sometimes mountains are so difficult that you throw up your hands in surrender and try to find a way around them. If you could avoid it, you would. In fact, many dance around their mountains or pretend as if they are not staring them in the face.

To others with a greater vision, mountains are opportunities waiting to be overcome, a uniquely placed, mere stepping stone to greater heights in life and discipline. You may see mountains as stubborn problems you have been trying to solve without much success. This might be a condition that hinders your progress in life, like an addiction that has held you hostage or a particular situation, domestic or workplace, secular or spiritual, academic or vocational.

Whatever your circumstance, it is definitely something you have been battling with either for a short or long time. Mountains are not necessarily a domestic nightmare, physical disability or spiritual disappointment; they could be mental torture or social stigma that looms over you like a gargantuan monster impeding your progress.

Some people see mountains as challenges that need to be overcome while others see a mountain as something to avoid as much as possible even if it means living the rest of their lives in the lowlands. Mountains can be problems and difficulties in the form of a gift-wrapped present delivered in a puzzle. Whatever the circumstances, we need to reach for higher heights in our life.

In this book, we will look at mountains, inter alia, as metaphors for opportunities, obstacles, challenges and hindrances to our life's destiny. We will approach it mainly in a spiritual, non-theoretical format with a bird's eye view of life to prepare ourselves to take on such challenges with confidence in the future. This approach is primarily Christ-based but I am convinced the facts and circumstances we will draw upon are relevant to people from all walks of life and types of faith. This is not just another religious book.

I am convinced many whose potential remains unfulfilled will find this book a cause for celebration. In the following pages, we will learn about obstacles to conquering mountains and how to overcome them. Regardless of your present circumstances or your confidence in your ability and potential, I am convinced that by the end of this book, you will not be content living in the lowlands. Instead you will discover the secret to reaching your very best, in spite of life's daily challenges, as you pursue your long-term hopes and dreams. Are you ready to step up and embark on your journey to the top of the mountain? Come with me...

PRINCIPLES

1. Mountains come in various shapes, sizes and degrees of notoriety. Admirers of majestic peaks gape in awe at their grandiose cliffs while others choose to ignore them.

2. Those who dare to ascend and descend these mountains understand the pain, hardship and difficulties they will endure along the way.

3. The metaphor of the regal and dour mountain is the story of man's quest to understand life as well as cultivate the earth's abundant resources for the benefit of mankind.

4. In the end, all mountains, bland or regal, are crowns on the head of those who dare to reach their summits and come back to tell the tale of their ascent and descent.

5. Mountain and rock climbing speak to our desire as human beings to reach beyond our physical and emotional limits, past morbid fear, fatigue and excruciating pain to get to the apex of our dreams.

6. There is a reason why the two opposing armies were encamped on two adjacent mountains during one of the most important battles in the Bible between David and Goliath. (I Samuel 17:3)

7. Both the Davids and Goliaths of this world will have to endure the excruciating hike up the mountain before the inevitable combat of destiny takes place.

8. No matter the advantage you bring to the battle, be it height, strength, or dexterity in handling weapons, you must first get to the top of your mountain before you get the chance to show the world your skills.

9. The purpose of mountains in our world is more spiritual than physical, as such, it is still important to note that these mountains exist because God put them there.

10. It is only those who are willing to persevere and reach deep into the core of their being that will reach the peak of their careers and destiny.

11. Whatever the mountain may be, Everest or Kilimanjaro, a mountain of debt or a mountain of lack, a mountain of work or a mountain of adversity, a mountain of sickness or a mountain of affliction, whether they appear intimidating or overwhelming, you need to summon within you the deep riches of heaven to overcome it.

12. To have a mountaintop experience, you have to go over the mountain.

13. Many often make the mistake of likening life to the ascent of one solitary mountain.

14. In the journey of life, there are as many mountains to climb as there are rivers to cross.

15. If you linger at the top of one mountain, the world will move on while you celebrate yesterday's victories.

16. Mountains can represent difficult challenges in our life or in the alternative, opportunities.

17. Mountains can be problems and difficulties in the form of a gift-wrapped present delivered in a puzzle.

18. Are you ready to step up and embark on your journey to the top of the mountain? Come with me...

DISCUSSION GUIDE

1. Discuss your understanding of mountainous challenges with your study group.

2. Make a list of life's mountainous challenges you have faced and are still facing in your life.

3. How do you perceive mountains in your life? Are they stepping stones or stumbling blocks?

4. Discuss your past experience in hiking actual physical hills and mountains.

5. Identify five common purposes of mountainous challenges.

6. Discuss with the group your list of life's besetting mountainous challenges and your plans for overcoming them.

The gospel of Christ liberates man from the pervasive ignorance of his environment.

CHAPTER TWO
MOUNTAINS THROUGH THE AGES:
OLD TESTAMENT MOUNTAINS

Thousands of tired, nerve-shaken, over-civilized people are beginning to find out going to the mountains is going home; that wilderness is a necessity...
— John Muir [1]

An understanding of mountains through the ages will prepare us for the task ahead of us. In the next two chapters, we will view mountains through the lens of the Bible and history. From time immemorial, people and cultures all over the world have seen mountains as mysteries and riddles, some to be avoided and others to be gazed upon from a distance. Some even worship mountains and turn them into gods with divine attributes.

Growing up in Africa, I often heard my paternal grandmother speak in awe of Idanre Hills. On a recent visit with my children to Olumo Rock, in Abeokuta, Ogun State, Nigeria, our tour guide regaled my "American-born children" with what the rocks meant to the Abeokuta people and the sacrifices that had to be made at its shrine if the entire town were to avoid the wrath of its volcanic ashes. One of my kids then tried to explain scientifically what causes volcanic eruptions and that it has little or nothing to do with the wrath of gods. The tour guide looked at her with puzzlement, turned aside and said something under his breath, like an incantation, and then proceeded with his job as if nothing was ever said.

I sensed his belief in the potency and power of that ancient rock was deep. The truth remains, that very often, what Africans can't explain they deify. Thank God for the gospel of Christ that has liberated man from this pervasive ignorance. It would be wrong to think that such belief is restricted to African Traditional Religion worshippers. As Richard D. Patterson said, "Ancient gods were at times associated with mountains as was the case with the Ugaritic god, Baal Zephon." [2]

I also recall growing up as a Roman Catholic altar boy, asking our Irish Catholic priest why we had to march to "Oke Maria" – Maria Mountain (located in southwest Nigeria) to see an apparition of Mary when he often taught us God is everywhere. I frequently asked him what made the church's annual Easter parade to Imo Hills near my hometown unique when God does not dwell in earthly structures but in the heart of man. He would often find a way to avoid answering my questions by claiming that there are many mysteries we do not understand.

This is as true today as it was in the time of the Old Testament children of Israel. Patterson writes that "Unfortunately, hills and mountains all too often became sources of Israel's idolatrous worship practices for which God's people were sternly reprimanded by God and his prophets." (e.g., 2 Kings 17:10-12; Jeremiah 2:20; 3:6) [3]

And yet, even until the present time, many still believe mountains and rocks are inhabited by dragons, demons and foul creatures. Mountains generally remain "terra incognita" – unperceivable, impassable and unknown lands for many generations. It was only when it became necessary to cross a mountain to find food, trade or for a pilgrimage that people started taking on the challenge of transcending mountains. A writer at Summitpost.org describes it this way: "This ignorance of most people had an important consequence for those who occasionally did need to cross the Alps. Those who live near mountains only know its lower ridges, where they grazed their herds, cultivate their crops and hunt." [4]

As knowledge and enlightenment increased more and more, people changed their views of mountains from a complete aversion to a desire to conquer and impose man's will against all odds. Wealthy citizens, poets and philosophers were the source of this change. Increasingly, people began to view the mountain summit as a place of exquisite beauty, gorgeous views and exotic beauty available for those who dare. [5] As John Muir once observed, "Thousands of tired, nerve-shaken, over-civilized people are beginning to find out going to the mountains is going home; that wilderness is a necessity..."[6] More and more scientific research and expeditions also succeeded in changing the common view of mountains as terra incognita.

In the Bible, mountains are mentioned frequently as an object of admiration, the desire of nations and a divinely exalted adventurous place worthy of pursuit

Every mountain, including the ones you are facing right now, must necessarily answer to the power and commandments of God.

as well as a metaphorical signpost for God's protection, hope imbuing and faith inspiring. A good example of this can be found in the book of Isaiah, "Now it shall come to pass in the latter days that the mountain of the Lord's house shall be established on the top of the mountains, and shall be exalted above the hills; and all nations shall flow to it. Many people shall come and say, "Come, and let us go up to the mountain of the Lord, To the house of the God of Jacob; He will teach us His ways, And we shall walk in His paths. For out of Zion shall go forth the law and the word of the Lord from Jerusalem." (Isaiah 2:2-3)

Other passages view mountains as a destructive evil that will be judged by God and burned. An example of this is in the book of Jeremiah, "Behold, I *am* against you, O destroying mountain, who destroys all the earth," says the Lord, "And I will stretch out my hand against you, Roll you down from the rocks, and make you a burnt mountain." (Jeremiah 51:25)

As a reminder, the two common words used for mountain in the Bible are "*har*" in Hebrew and "*oros*" in Greek. "The simple definition for each is mountain or hill, though they may indicate hill country or a mountainous region."[7] In the Bible, many important events took place in or near mountains. Patterson states that "Due to their durability, height, and make-up, they often became natural places for refuge and security, territorial boundaries, and strategic military locations."[8] In fact, the Psalmist in one of the Song of Ascent states, "Those who trust in the Lord are like Mount Zion, which cannot be moved but abides forever. As the mountains surround Jerusalem, so the Lord surrounds His people from this time forth and forever." (Psalm 125:1-2) Of all the metaphors in the world one can use to explain faith, Jesus Christ in Matthew 17:20 and Mark 11:23 used a mountain! Why? Could it be because the familiar topography of those assembled before him was dotted with mountains and hills and he needed something they could relate to?

As Christian writer, Joe Paprocki, (whom I owe much of the information in this chapter) clearly stated that mountains dotted the landscape of the geographical regions where the stories of the Bible took place. Mountains, therefore, not only played a significant symbolic role in the Bible but are also part of the physical reality of the lands described therein. As a result, mountains, hills and elevated landscape are mentioned over five hundred (500) times. God is often referred to as a Supreme Being who dwells in the heavens above. During Bible times, mountains thus had a logical religious symbolism. Very often God reveals himself on the mountaintop.[9]

In the New Testament, Jesus frequently took His disciples to the mountaintop even as He himself took time away on the mountain to contemplate, pray and meditate. He was tempted on a mountain (Matthew 4:8), He delivered the Beatitudes in His Sermon on the Mount (Matthew 5:1) and He healed "the lame, blind, mute, maimed and many others" on a mountain by the Sea of Galilee. (Matthew 15:30) His transfiguration took place on a high mountain where Jesus took Peter, James and John.

At that mountain, He had Moses and Elijah with Him, both of whom had also encountered God in the Old Testament on mountains; the latter at Mount Carmel and the former at Mount Sinai and Horeb among others. Moses was said to have been buried by God Himself on Mount Nebo, while Elijah ascended to heaven in a chariot of fire and a search party searched all the mountains in vain looking for his body and returned when they couldn't find him. Moses and Elijah herald the end of the law and the prophets. Jesus Christ also revealed signs of the end times to His disciples on the Mount of Olives. (Matthew 24:3) He commissioned His disciples for the Great Commission on a Galilean mountain He had appointed beforehand to His disciples. (Matthew 28:16)

OLD TESTAMENT MOUNTAINS

The first time a mountain is mentioned in the Bible is in relation to the fact that even mountains cannot evade the judgment and power of God. In Genesis 7:20, we learn that the flood in the time of Noah prevailed over every vertical object on earth and covered even the tallest of the mountains. This should be a thing of joy for everyone facing mountains of problems and challenges today. Every mountain, including the ones you are facing right now, must necessarily answer to the power and commandments of God. There is no mountain higher than God. In fact, He created the mountains and He can use whatever you are going through today to give you a fresh start, if you trust in Him. More importantly, it is instructive to note that in the two perfect chapters of the Bible, Genesis chapters one and two, where God said everything He created was good, there is no mention of any mountains.

MOUNT ARARAT

The next time a mountain was mentioned in the Bible was after the flood, and it was to remind us that Noah's ark of safety and protection rested on Mount Ararat, in the seventh month, on the seventeenth day of the month. God had divinely inspired Noah to build an ark of safety for himself, his wife, his sons and sons' wives as well as two (male and female) "of every living thing of all flesh." (Genesis 6:19) He intended to pass judgment on the earth by flood. The exact timing for the cessation of the flood is significant as seven is the number of completion. God's plan for Noah's safety and protection was surely completed by God. I don't know what He has said concerning you, but He will surely complete it.

The significance of Mount Ararat, located in present-day Turkey, can also not be overemphasized. This is the first named mountain in the Bible. The fact that Noah's ark rested on Mount Ararat also means that God's deliverance will not leave you at the foot of the hill but the top of your mountain of rest. The travails that you may be going through may have been induced by sin or self-driven but all you need to do is to obey His divine direction in your life and He will not only give you rest, He will set you down on the mountain of rest where you can enjoy the view. The first thing Noah and the inhabitants of the ark saw were not demons and foul spirits but the summits of the mountains all around them. God's plan for your life is to keep you and your family safe, while destruction may be going on all around you.

The secret to Noah's deliverance lies mainly in his obedience to the commandments of God. Noah obeyed God and prepared the ark according to God's word. He entered the ark with his entire family and God shut him in. He will not shut you in without delivering you safely to a mountain of rest and safety. I don't know the mountainous challenges you are facing today, but I do know that God will not abandon you. He will help you overcome every mountain of sorrow, disappointment, failure, depression, addiction, and every trial and tribulation towering over you like a gargantuan monster, if you will obey him. Jesus Christ said, "Come to me, all you who labor and are heavy laden, and I will give you rest." (Matthew 11:28) It is interesting that the first time the word "come" was used in the Bible it was in relation to God's call to Noah and his family to come into the ark. "Come thou and all thy house into the ark, for thee have I seen righteous before me in this generation." (Genesis 7:1) (KJV)

Just like in the day of Noah, He is still calling you today, "There remaineth therefore a rest to the people of God. For he that is entered into his rest, he also hath ceased from his own works, as God did from his. Let us labor therefore to enter into that rest, lest any man fall after the same example of unbelief." (Hebrews 4:9-11) (KJV)

The descendants of Noah didn't keep the covenant of obedience between Noah and God. As a result, they built the Tower of Babel and the Lord scattered them over the earth and confounded their language. (Genesis 11:1) One could argue that mountains did not feature in the life of early Bible dwellers because they were living atop mountains and they did not know the pains and struggles of mountain climbing; at least not until they journeyed from the East and found the plains in the land of Shinar and dwelt there.

It was from those plains they hatched the plan to build the Tower of Babel. "Come, let us build ourselves a city, and a tower whose top is in the heavens; let us make a name for ourselves, lest we be scattered abroad over the face of the whole earth." (Genesis 11:4) The tortured logic here is that they did not wish to be scattered abroad so they needed to make a name for themselves. The hubris and vain glory is self-evident.

Trials don't end just because you are relocated to the summit of a mountain or just because you conquer the enemy.

Mountain climbing can be sin-driven, self-driven, or Spirit-driven. We can also see that they started this self-absorbed pompous adventure from the plains, a place of relative comfort and peace. The mistake people often make is to think that things would have been different if they were not facing a certain mountainous problem in their life. Many even say once they are comfortable, all their mountainous problems will fly away. This is why the Bible warned those that stand, to take heed, lest they fall. (I Corinthians 10:12) The insatiable desire of man for vain glory often drives man to mountains and great ambition. Any ambition that is not divinely inspired is bound to end in heartache and confusion. But those who call on the name of the Lord shall not only be saved, they shall also not be moved.

ABRAHAM AND MOUNTAINS

Curiously, when next we read about mountains in the Bible, it is in relation to a man of covenant and faith, Abraham. In Genesis 12, the Lord asked Abram (as he was then known) to leave his homeland and go to the land which God would show him. He relocated Abraham (who decided to take his cousin, Lot, with him) to the mountains east of Bethel, where Abraham built an altar to the Lord, and called on the name of the Lord. (Genesis 12:8) In Genesis 13:14-16, Abraham had another conversation with the Lord after he had separated from Lot. God promised to make his descendants like the dust of the earth.

In the third recorded encounter between Abraham and God, we learn after Abraham defeated an invading army that had taken over the mountain of Seir and given a tithe of his spoils to Melchizedek king of Salem, "the word of the Lord came to Abram in a vision, saying, "Do not be afraid, Abram, I am your shield, your exceedingly great reward." (Genesis 15:1)

This is significant as this is the first time the phrase "the Word of the Lord" appears in the Bible. This time around the Word asked Abram not to look down at the dust but up at the stars in the heaven, and that as innumerable as the stars are, so shall his descendants be, even though at this time, Abram was childless. But the Bible says Abraham believed in the Lord and He accounted it to him for righteousness. There is an argument made that the "Word" that appeared to Abraham here is the same "Word" that existed at the beginning in John 1:1 (Jesus Christ). In fact, Jesus Christ himself said in John 8:54-58 when talking to the Jews, "Your father Abraham rejoiced to see My day, and he saw it and was glad." (John 8:56)

I am convinced that God accounted Abraham's belief in the invisible Christ for righteousness, because he trusted in God's power, provision and promise. When you see the invisible, you cannot be scared by the impossible. You, too, can believe in the invisible God to confront all the impossibilities in your life. His promises are sure and able. His promises are unlimited in ability and assurance. His promises are not hollow, because God is not dependent on anyone to fulfill His promises.

Politicians depend on voters, bankers depend on their investors' capital, or a government bailout, unions depend on their members' dues, charitable institutions depend on their donors, but God is not dependent on anyone for power, provision or capability. God is one hundred percent (100%) independent in His provision, power and grace. As we learn in John 1:3-4, "all things were made through him and without Him nothing was made that was made. In Him was life and the life was the light of men." (KJV)

It is interesting that everyone that acknowledges Christ and catches a glimpse of Christ in the Old Testament tends to have a special relationship with God.

David, a murderer and adulterer was said to be a man after God's own heart, why? We can see a glimpse of why God gave him such a special place in His heart, as we read Psalm 110:1, "The Lord said to my Lord, sit at my right hand, till I make your enemies your footstool." This was written thousands of years before Christ was born. David saw this revelation that mountains of life only become our footstool by the grace of Him who upholds all things by the word of His power, and who "when he had by Himself purged our sins, sat down at the right hand of the Majesty on high ... having become so much better...He has by inheritance obtained a more excellent name..." (Hebrews 1:3-4) Knowledge of that name and a relationship with the owner of that name is definitely crucial to overcoming life's mountainous challenges.

As we soon find out, trials don't end just because you are relocated to the summit of a mountain or just because you conquer the enemy. We learn in Genesis 22, that God tested Abram by commanding him to take his son, "your only son, Isaac, whom you love and go to the land of Moriah, and offer him there as a burnt offering on one of the mountains of which I shall tell you." (Genesis 22:2)

First of all, we see that mountain climbing can also be Spirit-driven, upon the commandment of the Lord. Second, this is the first time the word "love" is mentioned in the Bible; and it is in relation to sacrificial love, the agape kind of love, the same love that caused Christ to lay down His life for His brethren. Third, God addressed Isaac as Abraham's only son, even though biologically, Isaac was not Abram's only son, Ishmael was also a son and God indeed blessed him, too.

The lesson here is that as far as God is concerned, the spiritual covenant is what counts. Isaac is the child of the covenant between God and Abraham while Ishmael is a child born out of carnality. Even though God blessed Ishmael and made him great, God still honors Isaac as the recognized son of the covenant. God does take His promised covenant seriously. Whatever He promised you, He will surely accomplish and make it come to pass. Just as Christ, the only begotten son of God, was later sacrificed on the hill of Moriah at Calvary, Isaac was a foreshadowing of God's sacrificial love.

Much has been written about the faith of Abraham but little about the faith of the young man, Isaac. Abraham was 100 years old when Isaac was born (Genesis 21:5) and at the time of this trip, Isaac would have been at least 17 years of age. For such a young man to be able to withstand the long trip to the top of Mount Moriah is quite a feat. What is more, when his aging father bound him, laid him down on the altar and placed the wood around it in preparation for sacrificing him, the boy never struggled or ran away.

The victory of faith has little or nothing to do with age. We can call Mount Moriah, the mountain of faith and obedience, (Genesis 22:2) because it was here we first encountered a man with the shining evidence of good faith in God. (James 2:21-24) It was here he earned the title "Father of Faith" and "Friend of God". (Romans 4:16)

Interesting enough, it was the same Mount Moriah (including all the land around it) that David purchased from Ornan the Jebusite and built an altar for sacrifices. Solomon later built the temple on top of the mountain. (2 Chronicles 3:1) "Then Solomon began to build the house of the Lord at Jerusalem in Mount Moriah, where the Lord appeared unto David, his father, in the place that David had prepared in the threshing floor of Ornan, the Jebusite." There are clouds of witnesses who will be encouraged by our strong determination to surmount mountains where we can offer our lives as a living sacrifice to God.

MOUNT HOREB/MOUNT SINAI

Another spectacular mountain frequently mentioned in the Bible is Mount Horeb, also called Mount Sinai. This is the only mountain called the Mountain of God. According to Biblearchaeology.org, "Sixty three (63) chapters of the Old Testament are devoted to events that took place at Mount Sinai. This amounts to 14% of the 436 historical narrative chapters from Genesis to Esther. After Elijah's visit, Mount Sinai dropped out of biblical history, and its location faded from the remembrance of God's people." [10]

There is a reason why God made it undiscoverable, imagine if in today's tourist crazed world people knew there was a mountain where God appeared to Moses, not only would they build an altar there, many would even worship the mountain, forgetting that the God of Abraham, Isaac and Jacob does not dwell in earthly structures or mountains. However, the significance of Mount Sinai is even more subtle than we can imagine.

The first time Mount Sinai was mentioned in the Bible happened to be the first day of the third month of the deliverance of the children of Israel from Egypt. They encamped before Mount Sinai, and "Moses went up to God and the Lord called to him from the mountain." (Exodus 19:1-3) This is significant because there is a calling from God that comes when the journey to the mountain is Spirit-driven. Like Mount Horeb where Moses heard the call of God, this time around, God called the whole nation to prepare them for the journey ahead. Is God calling you to a mountain to prepare you for the task He has for you? Yield to His calling today and He will equip you with all that you need to get to your promised summit.

Moses receives God's instructions for Israel and delivers them to the people. Beginning with this passage, I found seven different instances when Moses had to go up mountains to receive instructions from God or plead for the people and then went down the mountain to address the Israelites. This is a repeated theme throughout the Mount Sinai experience.

As leaders, we must be ready to take the burden of God's people to the Mountain of God in prayer, and at the same time, come back down to explain the instructions from God. Seven, of course, as we noted earlier is the number of perfection and completeness. (Exodus 19:3, 20; 24:9, 13, 15, 18; 34:4) The eighth time Moses went up to the top of a mountain, Mount Nebo, God showed him all the Promised Land and he never came back. (Deuteronomy 34:1,5) Eight is the number of new beginnings and it is in the plan of God to begin anew with a new leader, Joshua.

God sometimes calls His people to the mountain to reveal our emptiness to us. And when He summoned the children of Israel to the Mountain of God, Sinai, it was not for fun, but for them to see His glory. When you see His glory on the mountain away from your lowlands folly, it will surely humble you. Whoever you are, and whatever your righteousness, will pale in insignificance on the Mountain of God's presence. As you see yourself in the light of His glory, all pride, arrogance and selfishness automatically flies out of you. If you humble yourself, He will open your eyes. What usually follows once you have been emptied of "me, myself and I" is mighty revelation.

Every encounter with the glory of God brings revelation. For instance, in Exodus 3:1-2, we learn that while Moses was keeping his father-in-law's flock, he came to the backside of the desert, particularly "to the mountain of God, even to Horeb; and the angel of the Lord appeared unto him in a flame of fire out of the midst of a bush."(KJV) God thereafter appeared to him and called him to a life of service. He was asked to stop caring for sheep and start caring for God's own pastures, God's chosen people. It was during this encounter that God revealed his name, "I AM THAT I AM" to Moses. (Exodus 3:14)

When we climb the Mountain of God caring for other people's sheep, He will reveal our deliverance and salvation to us. There on Mount Horeb, God revealed His intent and purpose to Moses, which was to deliver His people from Egypt. Moses would be an instrument in His hand to accomplish that purpose.

What is unique about this story is Moses' response. He gave all sorts of excuses why he shouldn't be the one that God would use. In the end, God convinced him by a miraculous display of His power.

He asked him, "What is in your hand?"

Moses said, "A rod."

Almost every nomadic cattle gatherer and shepherd has a rod. With that rod, they comfort and guide their flock. God displayed His power by asking Moses to put it down and it turned into a serpent. What appeared to be a small insignificant rod became an object of God's power.

There is something in your hand that God wants to turn into an instrument of His power. It might be your minimum wage job, your little children, your mortgage, your offering, your voice, your talents, your skills or your service; offer it up to God today and see Him turn it into a mighty battle axe, a never ending jar of oil or a rod that will part every Red Sea in your life. The sad thing here is if we refuse to go up to the mountain or even when we get to the mountain and we refuse to offer our rod to Him, not only will God not be able to use it to deliver His people, Satan may take it over and use it against us and God's people.

A lot of people wonder why I decided to start a free legal clinic at my church given how busy I am with five kids and my day job. I often tell people that I have to offer my little rod to God to use in helping people. After all, I would never have become an attorney in the first place but for His grace.

As the first lawyer in my family, the fact that I completed law school was a miracle. I lost my fairly well-to-do Dad during my sophomore year at the University. At the beginning of law school, I had no money to pay my tuition. In Nigeria, there is no access to student loans or grants that would have helped me. My mom had to pawn her clothes to pay part of my law school tuition and then took out a usury loan from one of my dad's brothers to pay the rest of it. In the end, I completed law school by the unfailing grace of God.

The victory of faith has little or nothing to do with age.

To Moses, Mount Horeb was first the Mountain of Calling before it became the Mountain of Instruction. Since the Garden of Eden, God had been looking for another opportunity to fellowship with the children of men. After delivering the children of Israel from slavery in Egypt, He asked Moses to summon them to Mount Sinai for an encounter with Him. Before then, only Moses had had an encounter with God, the children of Israel had only seen His acts of deliverance from the Egyptians. But for them to encounter God the way they were, He had to give Moses specific instructions on what they needed do, so they would not be consumed by the mighty and fiery glory of God on Mount Sinai.

The Mountain of Calling, Horeb, often changes to become the Mountain of Instruction, Sinai. A time of access to God is always a time for sanctification and dedication. You can't go to the Mountain of God without cleansing yourself. David said, "Who may ascend into the hill of the Lord? Or who may stand in His holy place? He who has clean hands and a pure heart, Who has not lifted up his soul to an idol, Nor sworn deceitfully. He shall receive the blessing from the Lord and righteousness from the God of his salvation. This is Jacob, the generation of those who seek Him. Who seek Your face." (Psalm 24:3-6)

Unfortunately, the children of Israel were ill-prepared for what came out of the mountain, even though Moses had followed God's instructions to consecrate them for the encounter. What follows in Exodus 19:16-20 is worth retelling in its entirety:

> "¹⁶ And it came to pass on the third day in the morning, that there were thunders and lightnings and·a thick cloud upon the mount, and the voice of the trumpet exceeding loud; so that all the people that was in the camp trembled.

¹⁷ And Moses brought forth the people out of the camp to meet with God; and they stood at the nether part of the mount.
¹⁸ And Mount Sinai was altogether on a smoke, because the LORD descended upon it in fire: and the smoke thereof ascended as the smoke of a furnace, and the whole mount quaked greatly.
¹⁹ And when the voice of the trumpet sounded long, and waxed louder and louder, Moses spake, and God answered him by a voice.
²⁰ And the LORD came down upon Mount Sinai, on the top of the mount: and the LORD called Moses up to the top of the mount; and Moses went up." (KJV)

Seven important things happened in this passage: (1) there was a massive display of God's Power. This could be seen through the thunder, lightning and thick cloud upon the mount. (2) The people stood at the foot of the mountain, even though they were brought out of their camp. (3) The glory of God was manifested in fire and smoke that descended on Mount Sinai. (4) The whole mountain quaked greatly. (5) The voice of the trumpet sounded long and waxed on top of the mountain. (6) Moses spoke and the Lord answered him. (7) The Lord came down upon Mount Sinai and called Moses up to the top and Moses went up. We need to examine this seriatim (one after another).

God will always display His awesomeness to those whom He summons to the mountain. As stated earlier, a mountain can be sin-driven, self-driven or Spirit-driven. When it is Spirit-driven, you must always get ready for a massive display of God's majesty. The beauty of His Holiness is forever displayed to those who are willing to pay the price and are ready to consecrate themselves.

Many are called, but few are chosen. Even though everyone was brought out of the camp to the foot of the mountain, very few people made it beyond the foot of the mountain. In verse 23, God told Moses that the people could not come up to Mount Sinai. Why? God asked Moses to consecrate the people and set a boundary between them and God's holy mountain (Exodus 19:10-13) because no impurities could go beyond the foot of the mountain of the Lord.

God asked Moses to bring Aaron. Even the priests could not go beyond the foot of the mountain. Some of them probably did not sanctify themselves as instructed. They felt they were too holy and sanctimonious to do what ordinary people were doing because the same instruction was given to everyone. Many men of God are denied entrance to the Mountain of God because of arrogance.

We later read in Numbers 3:4 that some of the priests died in the wilderness of Sinai for offering strange fires before the Lord. It is important that ministers of the Lord honor and venerate the work of the Lord. God's work must be done God's way not just any way that we please.

However, in the book of Hebrews, it is made clear that as New Testament believers we have a new mountain, one that can be touched unlike Sinai, and touched by the grace of Christ – the mediator of the new covenant. (Hebrews 12:22-24)

The manifestation of the glory of God in fire and smoke speaks to the New Testament warning that "our God is a consuming fire." (Hebrews 12:29) Fire is an interesting substance because it can consume, transform and make permanent, depending on the material going through the fire. No one can escape the fire of God. If you are a child of God, the fire of God is transmitting and transforming you into permanency. If you are not, one day the consuming fire will totally consume you. [11]

Whenever we hear the call of God and obey it, Horeb becomes Sinai in our lives. The same mountain where Moses was called is also the mountain where he received the two stone tablets on which the Ten Commandments were written. It is also on this mountain he received the complete instructions for the building of the tabernacle. Moses later built an altar to the Lord at the foot of the mountain and positioned young men to offer sacrifices to the Lord there. "Then he took the Book of the Covenant and read it in the hearing of the people" and meanwhile, the children of Israel were mouthing off approval and obeisance to the Word. (Exodus 24:7)

First, we need to understand that a nation and a people bedazzled by the glory, power and beauty of the Lord could not but agree with His divine instruction. Second, a covenant is made when God's word is heard and responded to. Our covenant with God is based solely on His words, His terms, not our own words and terms. [12]

Curiously, we later learn that Moses, Aaron, Nadab and Abihu went back up to the top of Mount Sinai and they saw a vision of God, "there was under His feet as it were a paved work of sapphire stone, and it was like the very heavens in its clarity." (Exodus 24:9-10) What they saw is as important as what they did in the presence of God; "so they saw God and they ate and drank."

God is always looking for fellowship with His people because He loves us. He may have dazzled the people with fire, smoke and lightning on the way to the mountain but at the summit, He has prepared a table for us. This was after all, His plan for creating man.

The angels were created in the strength of God but humans were made in the likeness of God. He did that because He craved to have intimacy and fellowship with us. No wonder on the mountaintop of God's power and majesty He is waiting to eat and drink with us. This is another reason why we need to endure the journey to the top. No matter the hardship on the way to the mountaintop, know that at the end of your trial and tribulation that the Lord is waiting to fellowship with you at the summit.

It was only at the end of this that the Lord spoke to Moses, "Come up to Me on the mountain and be there; and I will give you tablets of stone, and the law and commandments which I have written, that you may teach them." (Exodus

24:12) The Bible says Moses immediately arose with his assistant, Joshua, and went up to the Mountain of God. The important thing to note here is that until God teaches us we cannot teach others. Many ministers do not have time to wait on the Lord before bringing the word to God's people. I often admonish colleagues to understand that the church service is not the same as a sports event or country club. The people gather unto the Lord and not unto you. It is therefore incumbent on us, as ministers in the House of the Lord, to wait on the Lord's mountain to receive His Word for His people before mounting the rostrum to sermonize the people.

Moses went up only after putting Aaron and Hur in charge of the people. A lot of people, often in the guise of obeying God, neglect their family and the people they are asked to lead. Even though Aaron and Hur later proved themselves unreliable leaders of men, there was nothing in their past that would have made Moses doubt their leadership of the people.

The Bible says "the sight of the glory of the LORD *was* like a consuming fire on the top of the mountain in the eyes of the children of Israel. So Moses went into the midst of the cloud and went up into the mountain. And Moses was on the mountain forty days and forty nights." (Exodus 24:17-18) The radiant embers of God's glory are not meant to dazzle Moses but to remind the children of Israel of God's glorious presence and to help them trust what they could not see.

There have been times in our worship service at Spokane Dream Center when we have experienced God's glorious presence in such an awesome manner that we had to cancel our preplanned program and just worship at His feet. Even though we cannot see Him, He very often uses this to give us reason to trust Him.

The Ten Commandments were not the only thing Moses received on the mountain of the Lord. In fact, before hewing the stones on which the law was written, God gave Moses directions on how to build the Tabernacle of the Lord which includes the Ark of the Covenant as well as one of its most important components, the Mercy Seat. The Shekinah, or symbol of the Divine Presence, rested on the Mercy Seat. God knew the people would break the law and had already made provision in advance for their failure under the law. There is also in the pattern for the tabernacle, a table of showbread, which is meant to be eaten before the Lord.

Bread is necessary for survival and for fellowship. God's plan is to fellowship with His people even as He provides for their survival. Of course, the Bread also points to the Bread of Life – Christ. Moses was also given instructions to build a golden lampstand. Revelations 4:5 reminds us that the seven lamps on this lampstand represent the seven Spirits of God, which is the presence of the Holy Spirit in heaven.

Finally, God emphasized, again, that the tabernacle and its furnishings were to be built according to the specifically revealed pattern so as to reflect a proper representation of the heavenly reality.

So, we can see that at Sinai, God's holiness and unrelenting character was on full display and ready for action. One Christian writer sums it up this way, "During the Old Covenant, God was represented as One who could not be approached freely. Mount Sinai was a mount which had no access to the common Israelite. (Exodus 19:12-13) It demonstrated God's power to a rebellious and sinful people." [13] Ray Stedman pointed out the positives in all this. "This means that God can never be talked out of anything. God can never be bought off. We cannot get him to lower his standard … which is what we discover as we come into the experience of the Lordship of Christ." [14]

The problem with the tabernacle and the law, however, was that it only permitted a few people as representatives to come before the Lord. The common people could never come before Him. But nothing is essentially wrong with the law itself. The trouble, as Stedman again asserted, is with the tabernacle and the system of sacrifice which requires restricted access through the High Priest. [15] That is why the whole of Hebrews explains to us how to complete this reality. The book of Hebrews says, "Therefore, brethren, having boldness to enter the Holiest by the blood of Jesus, by a new and living way which He consecrated for us." (Hebrews 10:19-20) The tabernacle is a shadow of what is to come in the heart of the New Testament believer, and as Paul states in Romans 8, "there is therefore now no condemnation to those who are in Christ Jesus," we now have perfect access to the Father. This may explain the reason why no one could ever find the real Mount Sinai. The new tabernacle is in the body of the New Testament believer. (I Corinthians 3:6)

> **Mountain climbing can be sin-driven, self-driven, or Spirit-driven.**

Of course, the Mount of Instruction soon becomes the Mount of Intercession, as the children of Israel pressured Aaron to make a golden calf for them to worship when they couldn't wait for Moses to come back from the mountain. Their impatience drove them to idolatry, which of course, caused them to incur the wrath of Yahweh. John Wesley in his explanatory notes tells us that they were weary of waiting for the Promised Land. They thought themselves detained too long at Mount Sinai; though there they lay very safe and very easy, well fed and well taught, yet they were impatient to be going forward. They had a God that stayed with them and manifested His presence with them by the cloud; but this would not serve. They must have a God to go before them to the land flowing with milk and honey; they want to hasten to their reward and cannot stay to take their religion along with them. [16]

Please note that those that would anticipate God's counsel are commonly precipitate in their own. We must first wait for God's law before we receive His promises. He that believeth doth not make haste, not more haste than good speed.

Not only did God see what they did, He also knew the kind of people He was dealing with. He called them "stiff necked" which means obstinate, obdurate and disobedient people. At this point, God was willing to kindle His wrath against them and then raise offspring through Moses but here we see the unique leadership of Moses in calling for the mercy of God and pleading on behalf of the people. On the Mount of Intercession, you forget self and focus on others. The Bible says, "Moses returned to the Lord and said, "Oh, these people have committed a great sin, and have made for themselves a god of gold! Yet now, if You will forgive their sin – but if not, I pray, blot me out of Your book which you have written." (Exodus 32:31-32)

The unique thing here is that Moses' prayer of intercession first acknowledged the sin of the people. He did not try to shift the blame to Aaron, or some leaders, it was all the people. Second, he stood in the gap for the people. Even though God had promised to wipe them out and raise a new nation of promise from Moses, he did not allow "me, myself and I" to stand in the way of the people he was leading. Other leaders might have taken advantage of God's generous offer to Moses to raise a new nation through him with no thought for the people that surrounded him.

A prayer of intercession on the mountain is not the time to wallow in righteous indignation as some church leaders do when they pray for their nation. I have heard people put all the blame for the rot, decay and immorality of our country on Hollywood, Congress and unbelievers, generally, forgetting the many sins of believers themselves.

There are many churches in our world today that have regular prayer meetings. The divorce rate among Christians is as high as in the world. The rate of pornography clicks on the internet is as high in the Bible Belt as elsewhere. It isn't often that you will find five churches in the inner city in America with a significant evangelistic outreach program and those that have one will not be supported by others. And yet in arrogance, we seem to think that America's problems are due to the sins of unbelievers only! The earlier we start to intercede for the people's sin the better for us all.

Similar problems abound in the growing Christian population of Nigeria, Ghana and other developing countries. There are large congregations with hundreds of thousands of believers trooping to church on Sunday and yet, corruption, armed robberies, pen robberies (embezzlement), rape, idol worship, cultism and child abuse is on the rise. Many have spoken out against politicians who kneel down before men of God to get their minister's approval before an election and then donate millions of dollars in looted government funds to the church on Sunday while ministers of God keep silent in the pulpit.

Moses showed us a classic example of what to do on the Mount of Intercession and the Lord spared the nation as a result of his prayer. God indeed had mercy on his people and later separated Moses unto Himself to write another tablet of commandments. The Mount of Intercession again becomes the Mount of Separation.

Just as the Holy Spirit requested the disciples to separate Paul and Barnabas for the work of the ministry, Moses was separated unto the Lord for forty days and forty nights. At the end of this time, Moses came back with two tablets of testimony and a fiery shining face radiating the glory of God. So much so that he had to cover his face with a veil so he didn't frighten the people. For New Testament believers, the veil is broken through Christ.

Paul writing to the Corinthians said, "But if the ministry of death, written and engraved on stones was glorious, so that the children of Israel could not look steadily at the face of Moses because of the glory of his countenance, which glory was passing away, how will the ministry of the Spirit not be more glorious? For if the ministry of condemnation had glory, the ministry of righteousness exceeds much more in glory." (2 Corinthians 3:7-9)

ELIJAH

The next time we hear about Mount Sinai or Mount Horeb is in relation to another important prophet, Elijah. "So he arose, and ate and drank; and he went in the strength of that food forty days and forty nights as far as Horeb, the mountain of God." (I Kings 19:8) The background to the story will be fully explored in the section on Mount Carmel. Suffice it to say that Elijah at this time was being threatened by Jezebel and fled from her reach, running as far away south as Mount Horeb. Frederick Brotherton Meyer, a 19th century Baptist pastor and evangelist, wrote this about Elijah's sad state. "Up to that moment Elijah had been animated by a most splendid faith, because he had never lost sight of God. He endured as seeing Him who is invisible. Faith always thrives when God occupies the whole field of vision." [17] God used the wind, earthquake, fire, and ultimately, a still small voice to get Elijah trained to hear God's voice.

The lesson here is simple, "Let us refuse to look at circumstances, though they roll before us as a Red Sea and howl around us like a storm. Circumstances, natural impossibilities, difficulties, are nothing in the estimation of the soul that is occupied with God. They are as the small dust that settles on a scale, and is not considered in the measurement of weight." [18]

AARON AND HUR: THE HILLTOP OF TEAMWORK

Very rarely are hilltops mentioned in the Old Testament but there is one that stands out among all others. One Christian writer called it the hilltop of prayer but I choose to call it the hilltop of prayer, support and teamwork. In Exodus 17:8-16, the Amalekites declare war on the children of Israel. Joshua led the army into battle while Moses, Aaron and Hur went to the top of the hill.

The Bible says, "So it was, when Moses held up his hand, that Israel prevailed; and when he let down his hand, the Amalekites prevailed." When Moses' hands became heavy, Aaron and Hur supported his hands on opposite sides and Moses' hand became steady until the going down of the sun and the Amalekites were defeated.

This story is interesting in its perspective as it makes evident the need we have for one another and the sore need for teamwork. No one in particular could lay claim to the success of this battle as everyone including the army, the commander, Joshua; the spiritual leader, Moses, and his assistants, Aaron and Hur, all played significant roles in overcoming the enemy. In the New Testament, we are told that the early church was together in one accord and had everything in common as a result of which, the Lord added to the church daily those who were being saved. (Acts 2: 44-47) I believe the church worldwide will experience more miracles, breakthrough and massive evangelism, as we work together and network to help one another.

MOUNT NEBO

The next important mountain we encounter in the Bible is Mount Nebo, which is located in the mountains of Abarim. This mountain is unique because it is a place of vision and the eventual burial place of Moses. F. B. Meyer again wrote the following immortal words about Moses' experience on this mountain. "O men of God, get you up into the high mountain, from which you may obtain a good view of the glorious Land of Promise, and refuse to have your gaze diverted by men or things below." [19] Moses through an act of disobedience in the waters of Meribah-Kadesh was told that even though he could see the Promised Land from afar, he would not "cross over there." (Deuteronomy 34:4b) "Then Moses went up from the plains of Moab to Mount Nebo, to the top of Pisgah, which is across from Jericho. And the LORD showed him all the land…" (Deuteronomy 34:1)

The gospel of Christ liberates man from the pervasive ignorance of his environment.

The interesting thing to note here is that Moses at this time was one hundred and twenty (120) years old and he climbed the entire mountain from the plain to the zenith by himself, without any help from anyone. The Bible says, Moses' eyes were not dim, nor his natural vigor diminished. (Deuteronomy 34:7) God will renew our strength like that of an eagle. David said, "The Lord is the strength of my life." (Psalm 27:1b)

The Bible goes on to state, "So Moses the servant of the LORD died there in the land of Moab, according to the word of the LORD. And He buried him in a valley in the land of Moab, opposite Beth Peor; but no one knows his grave to this day." (Deuteronomy 34:5-6) Moses could not enter the Promised Land because of the sin of anger, something many of us consider minor. The writer of Romans warned us that the same judgment and severity of God can still be unleashed on the children of disobedience. "Therefore consider the goodness and severity of God; on those who fell, severity; but towards you, goodness, if you continue in His goodness. Otherwise you also will be cut off." (Romans 11:22)

The judgment of God comes not because God is mean but because He is serious. Moses served God diligently but he sinned. He was considered just in the sight of God and remained one of the meekest men that ever walked the earth, but forgiveness does not always carry with it the alleviation of the consequences of sin. We, however, have a better covenant but we should not continue in sin and expect grace to abound. He is as much a God of judgment as He is a Merciful God.

Robert Jamieson argued that the reason God concealed the burial place of Moses from everyone is to prevent the place from being ranked as "holy places and made the resort of superstitious pilgrims or idolatrous veneration, in after ages." [20]

JOSHUA

A mountain always offers protection against pursuers. After all, the name of the Lord is a strong tower and the righteous run into it and they are saved. When Joshua sent spies to Jericho, Rahab, the harlot, counseled the two men to "Get to the mountain." (Joshua 2:16) They hid on the mountain for three days until their pursuers gave up and returned to Jericho. Sometimes we have to run to the Mountain of Protection, our Lord Jesus Christ. It is in His name that we find safety and protection.

The story of Joshua is the history of the conquest and possession of the Promised Land. He took all the mountain country, all the lowlands, the plains and the mountains of Israel but curiously, we find in Joshua 11:22 that he left the Anakims alone, who inhabited the cities of Gaza, Gath and Ashdod. Even though the Lord had asked him to be of good courage and had promised him that "no man shall be able to stand before you all the days of your life" (Joshua 1:5), he was afraid of taking on the giants. So he tolerated them and they ended up tormenting the children of Israel until David and his mighty men took them on and defeated them.

MOUNT HEBRON

When my wife and I immigrated to the United States, one of the most important prayer points we brought with us was that God would build us a vacation house in my hometown. We usually wait on God (fast) at the end of every year, ever since we got married, and this particular prayer stood out like a sore thumb for more than ten years. We were convinced very early during one of those prayer times, that this prayer point had turned into a promise as we prayed, so we began to thank God for building this house for us.

At the time, our income was barely able to meet all our expenses, and as such, the finances to start such a project appeared like a gargantuan giant to us. Each time we put money together and sent it home, it went to other more pressing projects.

This was the situation until one day my little sister called to inform us that she would be getting married and she wanted us to bring all the kids even though we had no place to stay. She volunteered to supervise the building of the house, if we were ready. At the time, we had barely five hundred dollars in our account. About the same time, my pastor called to tell me that he would be traveling and needed me to bring the message to God's people.

In preparing the message, the Holy Spirit led me to Joshua, chapter 14, particularly to the stirring words of Caleb, the son of Jephunneh, who at a very old age, challenged Joshua to "Give me this mountain" (verse 12), speaking of Mount Hebron. At the end of the message, I found myself drawing on the courage of Caleb and I decided to take on the giant of lack.

The Lord prospered my wife and we called my sister and sent her the money to buy the land. I traveled to Nigeria around February before the wedding in December, the Lord miraculously provided all that we needed to complete the building where we had the wedding ceremony. Mount Hebron can also become your mountain of courage and possession if you are ready to be of good courage and trust the Lord to come through for you, even though there are giants all over the mountains that surround your inheritance.

It is significant to note that Hebron only became an inheritance of Caleb "because he wholly followed the Lord God of Israel." (Joshua 14:14) The giants were there but Caleb was not afraid, even though he was at an advanced age. There is only one thing that giants know to do, that is to intimidate you. We have to remember that we have the Lion of the tribe of Judah in our corner. All we need to do is to look unto Jesus for victory and He will overcome the giants for us. "Give me this mountain" means bring your problems to me because I have enough courage and faith in God to overcome the giants. Mount Hebron also means Mount of Communion – a place where we share Christ as our inheritance.

As we explained in the previous chapter, a mountain can also be an obstruction to your destiny. In I Samuel 17:3, we learn that the Philistines stood on a mountain on one side and the Israelite army stood on a mountain on the other side, with a valley between them. The Philistine giant, Goliath, terrorized Israel day and night for 40 days because no one was willing to fight him. David, a young man sent to provide food for his brothers, decided to step up and take on the challenge. He had just been anointed secretly by Samuel in Bethlehem. It is important to bear in mind that the anointing on our life will attract significant challenges. In fact, the size of your challenge is equal to the anointing and calling on your life because God will not put you in a battle you are ill-equipped to face.

As Dr. Myles Munroe once said, "Whatever God expects from you He has already injected in you, and whatever he demands from you He has already supplied in you." [21] What is more, the size of your challenge determines the size of your reward. Goliath is tailored-made for David. Goliath intimidates and creates fear, even while wearing a huge suit of armor. His greatest asset is his defense. All he has for an offensive weapon is a spear with a limited range.

David had faith in the God of Israel and lots of courage to boot. He built his faith on past testimonies about lions and bears. David stayed within his strength by taking off Saul's huge ammunition and defense. He trusted in the name of the Lord and ran towards the challenge rather than away from the challenge. David demonstrated great faith in the Lord and was handsomely rewarded with the defeat of Goliath. He shows us that every tenet of faith requires courage and not timidity. What are the Goliath-like mountains staring you down? I urge you to have faith in God and watch your enemies fall and flee before you today.

MOUNT ZION

Perhaps the most strategic of the mountains in the Old Testament is Mount Zion. This is because it features prominently in Jewish history and is also the place where Christ will judge all carnal men: "Then saviors shall come to Mount Zion. To judge the mountains of Esau, and the kingdom shall be the Lord's." (Obadiah 1:21) Mount Zion was first mentioned in II Samuel 5, where the Jebusites, who used to inhabit the land, derided David and his army saying "you shall not come in here; but the blind and the lame will repel you… nevertheless, David took the stronghold of Zion" (v.6-7) and turned it into the City of David. Solomon later built the ancient temple on top of the same mountain.

You may have been taunted by enemies who deride your past accomplishments and rely on their natural fortress to challenge you and your faith in God. It may be a disease that the medical doctor calls terminal. I want to assure you in accordance with the Word of God that "upon Mount Zion shall be deliverance, and there shall be holiness, and the House of Jacob shall possess their possessions." (Obadiah 1:17) (KJV)

Zion, as a mountain, has both unique physical properties as well as an enormous spiritual connotation. The name Zion was even extended in the Bible to refer to Jerusalem – the City of God, the land of Judah, and the entire nation of Israel. This figurative meaning also extends to the New Testament Church of Christ as heirs of God's spiritual kingdom. This spiritual connotation symbolizes the light and glory of the new covenant. [22]

The glory and triumph associated with this mountain is directly related to the many prophesies about Christ the Messiah in the Bible. In Revelation 14:1, John the Apostle beheld the Lamb of God standing on Mount Zion with one hundred and forty four thousand (144,000) disciples. He predicted a victorious church that would overcome all manner of hardship and pain to stand on Mount Zion triumphant with the Lord Jesus Christ leading them.

Growing up as a born again believer in Nigeria, we often avoided telling anyone we were fasting. So over time some Christian brothers and sisters found a way around the conundrum, a way to communicate this fact to their brethren. Initially, it used to bug me, because when I asked folks, "are you fasting?"

They would say, "We are on the mountain Zion." Some would even start singing, "We are on the mountain Zion, and we have come to worship God."

And I would say, "Why don't you just tell me if you are fasting or not?" Then one day, one of our brothers on campus at the University called me to one side and explained to me that in Joel 2:32, Mount Zion does not mean a literal mountain but a place of prayer for those who separate themselves to be used of the Lord. Those who are saved call on the name of Jesus and refuse to defile themselves.

Needless to say, that after that explanation I personally began to study all the passages that referenced Zion and I discovered a treasure trove. For instance, I found out that Peter refers to Christ as the cornerstone in Zion and those that trust in Him will never be put to shame. (I Peter 2:6) I found Mount Zion to be the mountain of deliverance, protection and the stronghold of God. It is also a Mountain of Hope for all nations that accept Christ and make the journey with Him to the end.

MOUNT CARMEL

And now we come to Mount Carmel, the mountain of combat and victory in the Bible. Patterson wrote, "As the highest peak in a mountain range that extends from the bay of Acre on the Mediterranean coast inland to the plains of Dothan, Mount Carmel's southwestern slopes were famed for their fertility (2 Chronicles 26:10) and majestic beauty (Song of Solomon 7:5-6)." Another Christian writer provides a vivid contemporary description, "the Carmel range of mountains is fifteen miles long, with its southern boundary in the Bay of Acre, near the modern city of Haifa. The foothills flow into the Plain of Esdraelon. The highest point is 1,810 feet, with a promontory thrusting into the Mediterranean Sea, opposite the Sea of Galilee. The mountains collect heavy dew, remaining green throughout the year which is unusual for Palestine." [23]

Two of the mountain passes through this range were scenes of well-known biblical events: Megiddo (2 Chronicles 35:22) and Taanach (Judges 5:19-22). [24] A lot has been written about Elijah's battle with the worshippers of Baal on Mount Carmel but none is as poignant as the narration of the Bible story in the late F. B. Meyer's book, "Elijah: The Secret of his Power". The daring, the faith, and the confidence of Elijah, as told in I Kings 18, commands the same attitude of all mountain climbers.

Elijah had a simple idea to settle the disagreement. The God that answered by fire would be the living God, whether it be Baal or Yahweh. Baal worshipers prayed to their god from morning till noon and no fire came. Elijah prayed a simple prayer in obedience to God, standing on God's promise, rendered in faith with glory to God and "Then the fire of the LORD fell, and consumed:

1. The burnt sacrifice (confirmation of God's acceptance, Christ was our "once and for all sacrifice" through which He made us acceptable to the beloved)
2. The wood (this represents the potential of the nation that has been held in bondage under Baal)
3. The stones (stubborn problems in our lives)
4. The dust (fleshly desires)
5. And licked up the water that was in the trench." (every tear of sadness in our lives will be wiped away on our victorious Mount Carmel) (I Kings 18:38)

When I preached a sermon on this passage in our local church in Spokane, some of the brethren who came forward for prayer said they had never seen the problems in their lives as a challenge of faith. They thought fighting the good fight of faith was confronting unbelievers to be born again, and also, enduring persecution. A lot of people have relied on what they perceived as settled popular opinion to run their lives but God is asking us to come back to Him and put Him first in our lives.

As Israel did in the times of Elijah, so many of us have compromised in our Christian walk today. Jezebel Baal rules our lives even though we claim to be God's people. We need to search every area of our lives that needs to be consumed by the fire of the Holy Spirit. Thanks be to God who causes us to triumph in Christ and gives us victory through our Lord Jesus Christ. (I Corinthians 15:57) The encounter between the 450 prophets of Baal and Elijah teaches us that one with God is a majority, and that God's will in this world will ultimately prevail, even if the majority of the so-called powerful and influential people in this world oppose His will. (Matthew 7:13-14) We should never allow ourselves to be disheartened and discomfited by our lonely stand for God's ethics and morality.

In the next chapter, we will see that some of the mountains mentioned here and others as well appeared in the ministry of our Lord Jesus Christ and his disciples.

PRINCIPLES

1. People and cultures all over the world have seen mountains as mysteries and riddles, some to be avoided and others to be gazed upon from a distance.

2. The gospel of Christ liberates man from the pervasive ignorance of his environment.

3. History shows that only when it became necessary to cross a mountain to find food, trade or for a pilgrimage that people started taking on the challenge of transcending mountains.

4. As knowledge and enlightenment increased more and more, people changed their view of mountains from a complete aversion to them into a desire to conquer and impose man's will against all odds.

5. In the Bible, mountains are mentioned frequently as an object of admiration, the desire of nations and a divinely exalted adventurous place worthy of pursuit as well as a metaphorical signpost for God's protection, hope imbuing and faith inspiring.

6. Of all the metaphors in the world one can use to explain faith, Jesus Christ in Matthew 17:20 and Mark 11:23 used a mountain!

7. Mountains dotted the landscape of the geographical regions where the stories of the Bible took place. Mountains, hills and elevated landscape are mentioned over five hundred (500) times.

8. The first time a mountain is mentioned in the Bible is in relation to the fact that even mountains cannot evade the judgment and power of God. (Genesis 7:20)

9. Noah's ark of safety and protection rested on Mount Ararat, in the seventh month, on the seventeenth day of the month.

10. The fact that Noah's ark rested on Mount Ararat also means that God's deliverance will not leave you at the foot of the hill but the top of your mountain of rest.

11. The victory of faith has little or nothing to do with age. We can call Mount Moriah, the mountain of faith and obedience (Genesis 22:2) because it is here we first encounter a man with the shining evidence of good faith in God.

12. As Christian leaders, we must be ready to take the burden of God's people to the Mountain of God in prayer, and at the same time, come back down to explain the instructions from God.

13. Every encounter with the glory of God brings revelation. When we climb the Mountain of God caring for other people's sheep, He will reveal our deliverance and salvation to us.

14. Zion, as a mountain, has both unique physical properties as well as an enormous spiritual connotation. The glory and triumph associated with this mountain is directly related to the many prophesies about Christ the Messiah in the Bible.

15. The daring, the faith, and the confidence of Elijah on Mount Carmel as told in II Kings 18 commands the same attitude of all serious mountain climbers.

DISCUSSION GUIDE

1. Discuss why many mountains remain mysterious until the Age of Enlightenment.

2. Have a discussion on the circumstances surrounding the first mention of 'mountain' in the Bible in Genesis 7:20.

3. Discuss Abraham's several journeys to mountains and their impact on his recognition as the Father of Faith.

4. What is the spiritual importance of Mount Sinai/Horeb to the New Testament believers?

5. Are you currently lifting up the hands of a Christian leader on the hilltop of teamwork? Are you willing to support the leadership if the limelight is not on you?

6. Discuss with your group the lessons of Mount Nebo to the ministry of Moses. How and why did the meekest man on earth fail to make it to the Promised Land?

7. Are there any areas of your life you need to rise up like Caleb and say "give me this mountain"?

8. Discuss the spiritual significance of Mount Zion to New Testament believers.

9. Discuss Elijah's battle with the prophets of Baal and its significance in your own daily challenge of faith.

"Mountain climbers know, see and hear more than those below in the valley. Those close enough will get to see the finer details of His appearance. Moreover, if God takes you higher, your problems become smaller."

–Pastor E. A. Adeboye

CHAPTER THREE
MOUNTAINS THROUGH THE AGES:
NEW TESTAMENT MOUNTAINS

With faith the size of a mustard seed, you can indeed move a mountain,
but you can hardly be expected to garnish your sandwich.
— Jarod Kintz [1]

As we move to the New Testament, mountains become a place of spiritual retreat and religious pastures. They are a place for prayer, trials, teaching, transfiguration and the final place of ascension for our Lord Jesus Christ. Most of these mountains were not specifically named so as not to put the focus on the mountain but on Christ. This is a good lesson for us. We often focus on our problems, forgetting our God is bigger than the mountains in our lives. The Psalmist says God established all physical mountains by His strength. (Psalm 65:6)

In the Sermon on the Mount, the Bible says, "And seeing the multitudes, He went up on a mountain, and when He was seated His disciples came to Him." (Matthew 5:1) The Bible here makes it poignantly clear that Jesus went to the mountain, ascended the summit of the mountain, first, leading by example, and then His disciples came to Him.

We have many leaders today that are not willing to pay the price of leadership. Montgomery Van Wart in his book, "Dynamics of Leadership in Public Service: Theory and Practice" retold the cynical story of a Frenchman sitting in a café who hears a disturbance, runs to the window, and cries: "There goes the mob. I am the leader. I must follow them!" [2]

In our day and age, this is the type of leadership we see in both secular and spiritual leadership but Jesus Christ showed us a more excellent way. He knew His very presence attracted the multitudes. Jesus could have chosen to take advantage of the large crowd and use them for his own selfish purposes like putting them to work to build a mansion for Him but He didn't. He withdrew from the crowds rather than follow their adulatory flatteries. Jesus withdrew to the mountains for a time of personal reflection and contemplation in addition to in-depth teaching with His disciples. It is also important to note that like Isaac and Abraham, the disciples followed their Master to climb the mountain. They saw Him seated at the summit and quickly realized an opportunity for in-depth lessons. We need to recognize our "kairos" moment; every opportunity to learn at the feet of Christ must and should always be seized and embraced. The reward, of course, is that the disciples heard the most important teaching in the history of mankind; now called the Beatitudes.

As Pastor E. A. Adeboye illustrated in his sermon on the process of mountain climbing, there are a number of lessons we can learn from the Sermon on the Mount: 1. Jesus Christ was at the summit of the mountain and He was not only teaching but He was the focus. The Bible says if Christ be lifted up, He will draw all men unto Himself. As ministers, we should never forget this. Christ is the message and should be the focus of every sermon. 2. He went up. He was from above and the Bible says He that is above, is above all. 3. The disciples joined Him at the summit. They went up voluntarily without Jesus commanding or compelling them. 4. The multitudes never left the foothills. They could see Jesus at the top surrounded by His disciples but they could not muster the energy and will to climb the mountain and join Christ. "Many are called but few are chosen." (Matthew 22:14) 5. The disciples reaped the rewards of the toil and hardship of climbing the mountain to meet Christ as they were able to see Jesus more closely. They also got to hear Jesus more clearly. They stood in a position to understand the mysteries of the kingdom more thoroughly.

Pastor E. A. Adeboye (to whom I owe much of this section) put it more succinctly in his sermon on mountain climbers, "Mountain climbers know, see and hear more than those below in the valley. Those close enough will get to see the finer details of His appearance. Moreover, if God takes you higher, your problems become smaller." [3] We may not know the exact name of the place where the Sermon on the Mount was delivered, what we do know is that it was a mountain of pasture, where the Good Shepherd fed His sheep with the Word of Life. The sermon has been quoted since then by Christians and non-Christians alike who are seeking peace in the world or just seeking righteousness and justice.

MOUNT OF TRANSFIGURATION

From the Sermon on the Mount, we move to the Mount of Transfiguration. Patterson sums up the importance of this mountain for us, "Although the precise mountain on which this amazing event took place is disputed, some maintaining the traditional location on Mount Tabor, while others favor Mount Hermon or Mount Meron in northwestern Galilee, the presentation of a record of this event in all three synoptic gospels underscores the authenticity of Jesus' transfiguration." [4] Whether it be Hermon or Tabor, we know one thing for sure that the two mountains figuratively rejoiced at the sight of Christ, as the Psalmist once exalted, "Tabor and Hermon shall rejoice in thy name." (Psalm 89:12)(KJV)

Patterson states that none of the synoptic authors were actually concerned with identifying the particular mountain on which the event took place, because the transfiguration, and not the location, is and should be the most significant and not the name of the mountain. [5] I believe there is a distinct possibility that the event happened on Mount Hermon, "a magnificent mountain, rising to a height of 9,232 feet." [6] The event itself speaks of divinely commanded blessings that come from the unity of the law, prophecy and mercy in Christ. As the Psalmist eloquently describes, "How good and how pleasant it is for brethren to dwell together in unity! It is like the precious oil upon the head, running down on the beard, the beard of Aaron, running down on the edge of his garments. It is like the dew of Hermon, descending upon the mountains of Zion; for there the Lord commanded the blessing – Life forevermore." (Psalm 133)

Transfiguration speaks to the completion of the promise of God to redeem mankind and give eternal life. Hermon is a snow-clad mountain year round and has abundant dew descending on it. (Psalm 133:3) Mount Hermon, which means "sacred mountain", also forms the northern boundary of the land that Israel took from the Amorites. It was regarded as sacred by the Canaanites who inhabited the land before the Israelites. That the God of Abraham, Isaac and Jacob overcame the god of the Canaanites makes the triumphant transfiguration more plausible on this mountain. "The snow at Mount Hermon is a major source of the Jordan River, and water from its slopes ultimately flows into the Dead Sea." [7] I believe the Mount of Transfiguration speaks to our blessings that come with unity in Christ and the authority of the believer.

The account of Jesus' transfiguration is well stated in the synoptic gospels of Matthew 17:1-8, Mark 9:2-8, and Luke 9:28-36. The account states that Jesus led Peter, James and John "up on a high mountain by themselves." (Matthew 17:1) We notice here again that Jesus led them. Anytime Jesus leads you, expect tremendous revelation, safety, protection and provision. The question is, why are only three of the disciples present? What happened to the other nine? Were they too tired to embark on the journey? We may never know. What we do know is that as soon as they arrived at the summit, "He was transfigured before them. His face shone like the sun, and His clothes became as white as the light." (Matthew 17:2)

Immediately, the three disciples knew they were about to witness history. They saw the glory of God in action. They heard God speak endearingly about His beloved son. (Matthew 17:5) When you climb the mountain with Christ by your side, you will see the invisible that will emboldened you to do the impossible. They saw Moses, Elijah and Christ transfigured before them.

It is instructive to point out that the Luke account clearly states that the purpose for the trip was prayer and it was while praying that Christ was transformed before them. This should underscore the importance of prayer in the life of mountain climbers. When we pray, our vision is transformed. We need to see the invisible as Paul stated, the things which are not seen are eternal while the things seen are temporal. (II Corinthians 4:18) (KJV)

Vision aids transformation. If you don't see yourself overcoming your mountain, it is very likely you will remain in the foothills. As Pastor Adeboye said, "If you can't see yourself ministering to thousands of people, it will not happen. When you climb a mountain you see more and you will want more. What you see is what you will become. It is what you constantly see that will transform you." [8]

David saw himself killing Goliath before it actually happened. Joseph saw his brethren bowing down before him in Canaan before it happened in Egypt. A journey to the top of the mountain with the Lord will bring your glorious future into divine clarity before you. These three disciples also experienced something else – they heard the voice of God.

Now let us move from the clarity of the vision to the clarity of the message. The next thing we discover from their experience is that when they saw Jesus talking with Moses and Elijah, they too started talking.

I always tell our congregation that I will not die but live to declare the counsel of God. Unlike the Old Testament believers, an encounter with the glory of God will not strike us dead but embolden and equip us for the ministry of evangelism. We, however, need to have an understanding of the event we are witnessing to know the appropriate things to say. Peter began to express his desire while talking about building three tabernacles. The tabernacle speaks of the law, so God had to interrupt him with the real purpose for the event which was the declaration of God's divine satisfaction with the Son's ministry of reconciliation. It was followed by a divine command to listen to the Son.

Patterson states, "In light of all that these three disciples had witnessed, how could their lives and relation to Jesus ever be the same again? They should now surely realize beyond any doubt that not only was Jesus their teacher, but truly the Christ, "the Son of the Living God." (Matthew 16:16) [9]

More importantly, however, an encounter on the Mount of Transfiguration will inevitably expose our emptiness and thus humble us. The Bible says they fell on their faces and were greatly afraid. No one who has a divine encounter on the mountain remains the same. A glimpse of divine glory on the mountain also enables us to bear the pain and endure the suffering of persecution that may come our way. (Hebrews 12:2) It also enabled these disciples to see the next move of God.

In the account in Mark, as they came back from the mountain, Peter was able to perceive that Jesus was Christ the Son of God. One could argue that without the journey to the Mount of Transfiguration, he may not have been able to know who Christ was. The trip enabled these three disciples to see the cover and protection the law and the prophets provide for the Son of Man. We will soon find out from the next mountain we will discuss that this mountaintop experience is not only crucial as an authoritative historical event but was also vital to the ministry and office of the disciples, "especially after the death and resurrection of Christ." [10]

As they were leaving the mountain, Christ instructed them not to tell anyone what they had seen until the Son of Man had risen from the dead. Peter took this to heart, as years later he wrote in II Peter 1:17-19 about his encounter with the Excellent Glory on the Holy Mountain.

MOUNT OF OLIVES

So far we have discussed unnamed high mountains in the New Testament but one particular mountain that is specifically named is the Mount of Olives. Alden writes that the Mount of Olives lies in a "ridge running parallel to the Kidron Valley, east of Jerusalem." [11] According to Kyle Campbell, physically, it was a sight to behold. "It rises to a height of 2,641 feet. A magnificent view of Jerusalem and the Jordan Valley can be seen from the summit. The mountain received its name from the dense olive groves which grow on it. Although the Mount of Olives is only mentioned once in the Old Testament, (Zechariah 14:4) it played a prominent part in the life of our Lord."[12]

Its special importance in Jesus' earthly ministry cannot be overemphasized just as its importance in our prophetic future. Zechariah prophesied that "His feet will stand on the Mount of Olives, which faces Jerusalem on the east and the Mount of Olives shall be split in two from east to west making a very large valley." (Zechariah 14:4)

Matthew's account of Jesus' triumphant entry into Jerusalem states that as Jesus drew near to Jerusalem, He sent two of His disciples out from Bethphage on the Mount of Olives to go secure a donkey for Him at a particular place. During the last week of His life on earth, Jesus taught His disciples concerning future events on the same mountain, especially at it related to His second coming.

After celebrating the Passover with His disciples, Jesus again went out to the Mount of Olives, (Matthew 26:30) particularly to one of the relief slopes of the mountain where we find the Garden of Gethsemane. Here He asked His disciples to watch and pray as He went a little farther to pray alone. This slope on the Mount of Olives was the place where Jesus was betrayed and arrested. He came back to the summit of the mountain for His post-resurrection ascension in Acts 1:7-12. There He gave His promise to the apostles that His kingdom would come with the Holy Spirit. (Acts 1:4-12)

Transfiguration speaks to the completion of the promise of God to redeem mankind and give eternal life.

With this promise and its subsequent fulfillment, those who wish to live with God now have the opportunity to abide with Him in the eternal purpose of His church. (Ephesians 3:8-13)[13] The promise of the Holy Spirit launched the church with power and purpose and since then the world has never be the same. It is not, however, just any kind of power we need; we need the power of the Holy Spirit to overcome every mountain in our life. (Zechariah 4:6)

Mount Calvary

Finally, we cannot but talk about Calvary Hill, also referred to as Mount Calvary, where Christ bled and died for our sins. He died in our place, He bore our disgrace. II Corinthians 5:21 says, "He hath made Him to be sin for us who knew no sin; that we might be made the righteousness of God in Him."(KJV)

There is one common theme for both the Old Testament and New Testament mountains that we have examined in the last two chapters. That is the enduring fact that none of them is bigger metaphorically or physically than God. Not only did God's people overcome their mountainous trials, they also moved from conquering one mountain to another. The question is which mountain are you on? This is a question we all must answer, "Which mountain do you stand on? Which one will be your stability? Will it be the mount of Christ's authority, the mount of God's power, the mount of hope, or maybe the mount of severity and judgment?" [14]

As you read this, if all you see around you is judgment and devastation, I have good news. There is a more excellent way. Jesus came and bore the severity of God's judgment and severed the impact of life's aches and pains on the cross of Calvary. He paid the price so you can surmount life's mountains of hardship by His grace. You will never climb the mountain of pain alone again. He died so you may have eternal life. He rose from the dead so you may live free of shame, guilt and pain.

PRINCIPLES

1. Mountains often appear in the New Testament as a place of spiritual retreat and religious pastures.

2. They are a place for prayer, trials, teaching, transfiguration and the final place of ascension for our Lord Jesus Christ.

3. Most of these mountains were not specifically named so as not to put the focus on the mountain but on Christ.

4. We often focus on our problems forgetting our God is bigger than the mountains in our lives.

5. We may not know the exact name of the place where the Sermon on the Mount was delivered, what we do know is that it was a mountain of pasture, where the Good Shepherd fed His sheep with the Word of Life.

6. Transfiguration speaks to the completion of the promise of God to redeem mankind and give eternal life.

7. Vision aids transformation. If you don't see yourself overcoming your mountain, it is very likely you will remain in the foothills.

8. An encounter on the Mount of Transfiguration will inevitably expose our emptiness and thus humble us.

9. The Mount of Olives is the place where Jesus was betrayed and arrested. He came back to the summit of the mountain for His post-resurrection ascension in Acts 1:7-12.

10. The Mount of Olives is also where He gave His promise to the apostles that His kingdom would come with the Holy Spirit. (Acts 1:4-12)

11. Mount Calvary is where Christ bled and died for our sins. He died in our place, He bore our disgrace. (II Corinthians 5:21)

12. No mountain is bigger than God, metaphorically or physically.

13. In all the scriptures, not only did God's people overcome their mountainous trials, they also moved from conquering one mountain to another.

14. The question is which mountain are you on? This is a question we all must answer.

DISCUSSION GUIDE

1. Which mountain do you stand on? Which one will be your stability? Will it be the mount of Christ's authority, the mount of God's power, the mount of hope, or maybe the mount of severity and judgment?

2. Are you putting too much focus on the mountains in your life when Christ should be the center?

3. Do you see yourself overcoming your mountains or defeated and abused by them?

4. Examine your life. Have you stayed too long on the summit of one mountain when other challenges beckon you?

5. Are you afraid to come down from a conquered mountain because you are scared about the next challenge?

PART II
PLANNING, PREPARATION AND EQUIPMENT

We are called to endure and persevere in climbing some of the mountains of learning in our lives, such as the mountain of hard work and the daily grind of life. While on the other hand, we cast out and destroy demonic mountains of affliction.

CHAPTER FOUR
BETWEEN MOUNTAIN-MOVING FAITH AND MOUNTAIN-CLIMBING CHRISTIANS

The Philistines stood on a mountain on the one side and Israel stood on a mountain on the other side: and there was a valley between them. And there went out a champion out of the camp of the Philistines, named Goliath ... David hastened and ran toward the army to meet the Philistine ... And when the Philistines saw that their champion was dead, they fled.
– I Samuel 17:3-4a, 48b, 51b (KJV)

During the winter of 2012, I was unhappy and depressed. I was unhappy with everything. I was unhappy with my job, an area of my life that used to bring me joy. I felt I was not making as much impact as I would like to have on my clients as a lawyer and public defender. I was unhappy with my family life, as my wife and I were having too many arguments over what we later realized were trifling issues. I was unhappy with my son's asthma sickness which had grown progressively worse. I was unhappy with my spiritual journey with Christ, as I was disappointed with someone in the faith I held very dear. It was over an issue I should never have allowed to fester if I had been a better communicator. I was unhappy with my finances, as my wife and I owed a huge credit card debt we had incurred to provide for our extended family in Nigeria. In short, I was unhappy with my personal life, my finances, my secular job, and most importantly, my spiritual life.

My wife suggested that we fast and pray. I tried it for a couple of days and told her I really didn't feel like praying, she was shocked. She had never seen me so depressed since we started our journey together over 14 years ago. I personally could not recall if I had ever felt so bad. In fact, it was so bad, I could not stand me! I was disgruntled, irrational, grumpy and unhappy, snarling and screaming at anyone and everyone as if they were responsible for my miserable state. Eventually my wife could not take it anymore, so she forced me to take a week's vacation to visit her sister in New York hoping that a change of environment would at least change my mood. I reluctantly agreed. On the flight to New York, I was still sulking and feeling dejected.

My wife's brother-in-law, who is also a pastor with the Redeemed Christian Church of God, picked us up at the airport. He, as usual, was funny and lively and cheered me up a little bit. He told us that his church was having a unique prayer telethon where folks dialed in to a 1-800 teleconference to pray. We agreed to join them since we really needed all the prayer we could get.

The first day was amazing and the second and the third. By the time we left New York, we couldn't stop. After we returned home, we joined them in prayer until the end of the year. The more I prayed, the more relieved I felt. I could literally feel my faith increase by leaps and bounds. With my brother-in-law's quirky sense of humor still lifting my mood, we left New York happy and joyful.

The funny thing is that in none of the prayer meetings did we pray for ourselves. We concentrated on praying for the needs of the church and others. I came back loving my job and my family more. My ministry completely changed overnight. When I sat down to prepare a message, I found it easy to understand the Word of God. I never struggled through my messages again.

My senior pastor was so taken aback by this remarkable turnaround she decided to "re-preach" some of my messages during the Sunday morning service so more people would be blessed. I began to have a love relationship with the Word of God. I still listened to "tons of messages" but the urgency to cram every note I had into a forty-five minute message no longer gripped me.

I love the Lord enough to trust Him to speak through me. What is more, the more I pray for others the more the love of God gets shared abroad in my heart. Suddenly, I discovered that more testimonies followed when I prayed for others. Church members were giving me feedback about what God did in their lives when we prayed together.

Look at life's mountainous challenges as doors that need to be opened by faith, as well as a well-worn path and arduous task that need to be endured and persevered.

In short, those exciting times led me to write this book. Earlier I mentioned that this book was inspired by two sermons I listened to online during our trip to New York. My wife and her sister were gone to the hair salon. Our host pastor was at the church office preparing his Sunday sermon, so I was home alone with my iPad. My choices were watching English soccer on the cable channel or listening to messages on my iPad. But as God would have it, the Holy Spirit nudged me away from the soccer game.

I opened up my iPad and started listening to the messages of Pastor E. A. Adeboye and Bishop Mensah Otabil. The two messages had 'mountain' in the title so I was curious to find out how they each approached the topic. As someone later told me, these messages appear to be diametrically opposed to each other, at least at a cursory glance. Pastor Enoch Adejare Adeboye took the text of his message entitled, "Mountain Climbers and the Process of Mountain Climbing from Matthew 5:1-12, while Dr. Mensah Otabil took the text of his message entitled "Mountain Moving Faith" from Mark 11:22-24. [1]

Matthew chapter five is the famous Sermon on the Mount which contains the Beatitudes. Pastor Adeboye's emphasis, however, is on the first two verses of the chapter. "And seeing the multitudes, He went up on a mountain, and when He was seated His disciples came to Him. Then He opened His mouth and taught them saying." (Matthew 5:1-2) Pastor Adeboye started out by singing a very popular song among Christians in Africa. The song lyrics go, "I am going higher. Yes, I am. I am going higher each day. I am going to Jesus to stay. I am going above the shadows, into the presence of God, into the presence of Jesus. I am going higher each day." [2]

From the lyrics of the song, it is evident that the sermon's focus was on the daily Christian life marked by perseverance, endurance and longsuffering aided by the grace of God and the defining presence of Christ who has gone before us. He emphasized the fact that only the disciples summoned up enough courage to endure the trip to meet Jesus at the summit. And they are the only ones that got to see, hear and know Jesus more intimately. Even among the twelve, only three disciples made it to the Mount of Transfiguration. He went on to restate all the advantages of climbing higher with Christ. "To climb with Jesus, you have to lift up your eyes to see him who has gone before you, set your goal early, shed some weight (mostly sins), focus on Christ and press on, enduring shame and hardness with the help of Christ through prayer." [3]

Bishop Mensah Otabil, on the other hand, focused on Christ's admonition to His disciples after He had cursed a fig tree and it withered and they wondered how He did it. In Mark 11:22b-24, Jesus Christ said, "Have faith in God. For assuredly, I say to you, whoever says to this mountain, 'Be removed and be cast into the sea,' and does not doubt in his heart, but believes that those things he says will be done, he will have whatever he says. Therefore I say to you, whatever things you ask when you pray, believe that you receive them, and you will have them."

He explained that the Christian life is a life of the supernatural where we learn to use God's power to move mountains by faith. He went on to define faith as the substance of your expectations and evidence of the invisible. He encouraged his listeners to consider God's word as more real than what we see and to speak to every hindrance in the form of mountains in our lives in faith to move.

To deal with doubt, he encouraged everyone to ground their faith in God's goodness and generosity, surround our minds with God's promises, confess God's words and have an expectation that God will perform what He promised. Above all, we are to trust in God's sovereign wisdom, keep alert in the Spirit and wait patiently for the manifestation of His promise.

I listened to these two messages back to back, several times, sometimes one after the other. At first I got flummoxed by the differing directions each speaker took in approaching the topic. About the only thing in common was that mountains are stubborn problems in our lives. So I prayed and with the help of the Holy Spirit began a journey that led me to overcome the mountain of difficulty in understanding the two sermons.

In the end, I found the two sermons complementary instead of antithetical to each other. First of all, the same Jesus who climbed the mountain to separate

Himself from the multitudes is the same one who said we should say to "this" mountain "be removed and cast into the sea." It is self-evident that some mountains need to be climbed to separate us unto Christ. Jesus Christ said, "If anyone desires to come after Me, let him deny himself, and take up his cross, and follow Me." (Matthew 16:24) On the other hand, there are some specific mountains that need to be moved by faith. It may be because climbing them is not worth the effort or their mountaintop is not meant for us. The best approach for such mountains is total destruction. When a mountain is cast into the sea, the sea water dissolves it completely. It becomes submerged by the sea. The mountain exists no more.

We are called to endure and persevere in climbing some of the mountains of learning in our lives, such as the mountain of hard work and the daily grind of life. While on the other hand, we cast out and destroy demonic mountains of affliction. But in the same vein, there will be circumstances when your mountain of perseverance is beyond your capacity and your mountains of affliction need to be endured so you can learn the statutes of God. (Psalm 119:71)

The two are not mutually exclusive, nor do they necessarily work hand in hand all the time. What you need to do is to rely on God's capability, trust in His promise that He will never leave you nor forsake you. Follow His command to cast your net out into the sea by having the faith of God, while you continue to "work out your own salvation with fear and trembling as you climb up the mountaintop." (Philippians 2:12)

The truth is those who work out their faith with fear and trembling, often tend to have the faith of God that moves mountains. And those who move their mountains will often have climbed other mountains in the past or will move on to climbing more mountains in the future. The most important thing is to trust in God's divine direction for our lives.

No matter how you look at it, the two modes of overcoming mountains require faith in God. Faith is based on certain realities, the reality of God's power, provision and promise. You have to consider God's words as real in your circumstances. All of which comes down to the fact that you have read, seen and understand the Word of God. There is no other place to study the Word of God than to ascend unto the mountain with Christ. It is in the presence of God that we are transformed by the Word of God. After all, Christ is the Word of God. Great faith means understanding who Christ is and acknowledging Him as Lord over every circumstance. The more we look to God the more our burdens diminish in His presence.

One way to explain these two passages is by using the analogy of a beautiful house located at the summit of the highest mountain within a conclave of mountains. The head of the household has invited you to come to him anytime. It is an open invitation. Your goal is to reach the house and get all the benefits that a mountaintop experience can give you. The mountains have different local reliefs and different elevation levels. Some of the jagged edges and farthest reaches of the mountains have difficult terrains, too difficult for human mountain climbers. To these mountains, you say, "Be cast away into the sea!"

You need to know that the mountain may not necessarily physically move as that would cause a lot of destruction especially if the mountain is not anywhere near the sea. But figuratively, the mountain will cease to be an obstacle, as God will give you a special enablement to make it disappear miraculously. Remember it is whatever things you ask when you pray, believe you receive them, and you will have them. (Mark 11:24)

When you get past the jagged edged mountains and the uninhabitable hindrance, you will have to climb the mountain that will take you to the fortress of the Prince of Peace. On the way up, you will notice that sometimes God miraculously moves the mountain for you when you trust and have faith in Him. Many other times, though, He makes us climb the mountain of trials, pain and much suffering which demands a lot of hard work, grit and determination to facilitate growth and change in us.

Often the path we choose to reach the summit where the fortress lies is a well-worn path made straight by the One who has gone before us. Even though sometimes we would like to take a super shortcut that our brain tells us is quicker, God often alters our best laid plans. No matter how simple or complex, tedious or easy our path to the zenith may prove to be, we need to be humble and obedient to walk on His well-worn path and not the path the enticing words of men's wisdom desire for us to walk. Remember, He alone sees the end from the beginning.

At the fortress, the gates open automatically. We do not need a key to enter, as Christ has paid it all for us. (Hebrews 9:12) It is one thing to enter the compound and it is another to move through all the rooms in the castle, especially the ones with a good view. We, of course, have to enter the main house. The only key needed to enter any of the rooms in the fortress is the name of Jesus. (Philippians 2:10) But many after using the name of Jesus remain standing by the door waiting for the door to open. They forget that the door will only open when you act in faith and turn the doorknob. In James 2:26, it says, "For as the body without the spirit is dead, so faith without works is dead, also."

Know your source, assess what you have, understand the challenges before you and speak life into your situation.

In the Hall of Faith chapter (Hebrews 11), we read repeatedly how people by faith took steps to advance their divinely ordained destiny. For instance, by faith, Abraham "obeyed", "dwelt in the land of promise", "waited for a city". (Hebrews 11:8-10) By faith, Moses "refused", "forsook Egypt" and "kept the Passover". (Hebrews 11:23-28) Faith requires an overt, conscious act or denial to pursue your divine destiny to the detriment of all others.

Upon entering, you will be ushered into His presence with thanksgiving. By the time you enter the presence of the King of kings, as Bishop Otabil explains, all your concerns are swept away by the aura of His presence. In His presence is fullness of joy and at His right hand, are pleasures forevermore. All you want to do is worship Him. And all your mountainous problems recede and fade away in His presence.

The first thing that happens in His presence is the call and summons of God. We all must accept His gift and offer of help if we are to be overcomers in this life. No matter how powerful God may appear to you, if you don't personally accept His offer of help, the power will not be made available to you. His power counts for nothing in your life, if you shun Him.

As you will notice throughout this book, sometimes God miraculously moves mountains to get us to our destiny when we trust and have faith in Him. Other times, He makes us climb the mountain of trials, pain and much suffering which will require us to put in a lot of hard work, grit and toil with the resulting growth and inevitable attitudinal change in us. Very often the path we choose to reach the summit may not necessarily be the path He wants us to take. He sometimes rearranges our lives to give us the best view on "Experience" mountain. No matter the road we take, simple or complex, smooth or rough, plain or crooked; we must never forget that He will lead us back home.

We must be humble and obedient enough to understand that God is not programmed software on our GPS but the living God who sees the end from the beginning. He is the author and finisher of our faith. When we know that God is behind us, in front of us and by our side, it is a lot easier to follow His path for our lives. When we go through trials and tribulations, He will find a way out of the trials and tribulations, even while He teaches us life's greatest lessons in the process.

The best way to deal with crisis as we make our way to the summit is to begin with God and move on with Him. We must always look at life's mountainous challenges as doors that need to be opened by faith so we can see the face of God in every crisis. We can then stand at the door as He beckons us to stand in His light that will inevitably illuminate our hearts. Always use your mountainous challenges to find God in every crisis.

PRINCIPLES

1. The more you pray for others, the more the love of God gets shed abroad in your heart.

2. Only the disciples that endure the hike up the mountain get the view and only then do they get to talk with Jesus one-on-one.

3. Even among the twelve, only three disciples made it to the Mount of Transfiguration.

4. To climb with Jesus, you have to lift up your eyes to see Him who has gone before you, set your goal early, shed some weight (mostly sins), focus on Christ and press on, enduring shame and hardness with the help of Christ through prayer.

5. The Christian life is a life of the supernatural where we learn to use God's power to move mountains by faith.

6. Faith is the substance of your expectations and evidence of the invisible.

7. To deal with doubt, you need to ground your faith in God's goodness and generosity, surround your mind with God's promises, confess God's words and have an expectation that God will perform what He promised.

8. Trust in God's sovereign wisdom, keep alert in the Spirit and wait patiently for the manifestation of His promise.

9. The same Jesus who climbed the mountain to separate Himself from the multitudes is the same one who said we should say to "this" mountain "be removed and cast into the sea."

10. It is self-evident that some mountains need to be climbed to separate us unto Christ.

11. On the other hand, there are specific mountains that need to be moved by faith.

12. We are called to endure and persevere in climbing some of the mountains of learning in our lives, such as the mountain of hard work and the daily grind of life; while on the other hand, we cast out and destroy demonic mountains of affliction.

13. There will be circumstances when your mountain of perseverance is beyond your capacity and your mountains of affliction need to be endured so you can learn the statutes of God. (Psalm 119:71)

14. Those who work out their faith with fear and trembling often tend to have the faith of God that moves mountains.

15. Those that move their mountains will often have climbed other mountains in the past or will move on to climbing more mountains in the future.

16. The most important thing is to have faith and trust God for divine direction and instruction in our lives.

17. Be humble and obedient enough to understand that God is not programmed software on our GPS but the living God who sees the end from the beginning.

18. The best way to deal with crisis as we make our way to the summit is to begin with God and move on with Him.

19. Look at life's mountainous challenges as doors that need to be opened by faith.

DISCUSSION GUIDE

1. Have a discussion about individual mountainous challenges and pray for God's direction about the best approach to surmount them.

2. What are the necessary ingredients of mountain-moving faith?

3. Are perseverance and endurance necessary virtues for New Testament believers?

4. Share testimonies with your group about how God has brought you through crisis in your past.

"Peak performers want more than merely to win the next game. They see all the way to the championship. They have a long-range goal that inspires commitment and action."

— *Charles Garfield, Peak Performer*

CHAPTER FIVE
WHERE PREPARATION MEETS ASPIRATIONS:
THE SOURCE FACTOR

It's a tough lesson: There is no summit that comes before you expect it.
–Mark Obsmascik [1]

When I first asked my rock climbing buddy why he was so successful in the sport of rock climbing, he looked at me intently, smiled and said, "Look, it all comes down to vision, preparation, planning, and then, more planning." Successful mountain climbers put a lot of effort into preparation. They do not allow their aspirations to trick them into thinking the mountain before them is a cakewalk or a "walk in the park". My friend has climbed virtually every formidable rock in every state in the Continental United States. I am often amazed at the amount of effort he puts into preparing for a rock climbing trip. He often starts his preparation months ahead of time by searching for every little bit of information he can find about the rock, the location, the drive and the entire trip.

There is no doubt that proper preparation prevents poor performance. When you are faced with an enormous mountainous challenge, the amount of preparation you put into such challenge often has a great influence on the outcome. There is no doubt that when preparation meets opportunity, success is inevitable. More succinctly, Henry Hartman is quoted as saying, "Success always comes when preparation meets opportunity." [2] To be successful, therefore, we should always prepare for opportunities that are yet to come. Failure in life is not necessarily due to a lack of opportunity, but a lack of preparation. Most people fail in life because they are not ready when opportunity knocks. The good thing is, you can control how prepared you are but you can't control most of your opportunities. You have the power to prepare for the unknown with confidence.

As we will soon see, the same discipline required to navigate the mundane things of life is also what you will need to summon to surmount life's mountainous challenges, albeit with a greater intensity. Throughout history and the Bible, it is only those who are prepared that get to the top of the mountain. David conquered Goliath because he learned from his experience fighting and killing the bear and the lion. His preparation for the battle with Goliath was honed in the back desert fighting the bears and lions that tried to steal his parents' "few sheep" put in his care. (I Samuel 17:34-36) For the sake of one sheep, David risked his life and confronted a hungry lion. No wonder God could readily entrust him with the "sheep of his pastures" – the nation of Israel, because he never abandoned those "few sheep" even after Samuel anointed him king. He never abandoned those "few sheep" even for a good cause.

When his father summoned him to go and deliver food to his three oldest brothers and their commander in battle, he woke up very early in the morning and found a shepherd to take care of the sheep while he was away. (I Samuel 17:20) We can contrast that with an event in the life of King Saul, who was put in charge of his father's donkeys. When they strayed, he searched for them for a little while and then went home alone to his father, whom he felt must now be looking for him. Saul had no idea that he could seek spiritual help to locate the donkeys. In fact, his servant, probably a stranger to the covenant of Abraham, had to remind him to seek the help of a man of God who lived nearby. The servant even promised to loan him money to give to the man of God. (I Samuel 9:3-10)

"The very essence of leadership is that you have to have vision. It's got to be a vision you articulate clearly and forcefully on every occasion. You can't blow an uncertain trumpet."—
Father Theodore Hesburgh

The big difference between the failure of King Saul and the success of King David is preparation. You have to invest in yourself before others will entrust you with their investment. A call or summons from someone at the top of the mountain is not a substitute for preparation. It is a signal to prepare yourself to go up. When you feel an urge to do something, take a deep breath and start planning. Most often, that precise moment is not necessarily an opportune time to act but instead a call to prepare. The downtime between your calling and execution should be spent in prayer, meditation and preparation. Start reading books on the subject, then get to know those who have had similar challenges, and finally, get hold of useful tools for the journey at hand. Paul admonished Timothy to study to show himself approved unto God, a workman who does not need to be ashamed but rightly dividing the word of truth. (II Timothy 2:15) Daniel first learned by studying the Word of God and then he launched himself into praying and fasting for the deliverance of his people from Babylonian slavery. (Daniel 9:2)

Preparation starts with vision. Aspire to become something bigger than your mountain. Your destiny will be shaped by the vision in your heart. What you see in your spirit is what you will receive in material reality. You can never rise beyond your inner vision. Your past failures do not dictate what you will become if you apply yourself. Vision helps you answer the question of who you want to be. The capacity to imagine through the "eye of the spirit" will enable you to see victory over your mountainous challenge before you take the first step. If you see yourself defeated before you take the first step, chances are that you may never make it to the top of the mountain. The worst captivity is that of the mind.

In the Bible, two animals stand out as victorious leaders: the eagle and the lion. No animal has optical power like the eagle. When an eagle decides to focus on an object, the eagle's eye changes and the object becomes its primary focus while everything else becomes a blur and pales in insignificance. Vision, is therefore, clearly related to focus.

Preparation also starts with goal setting. Goal setting helps you focus on the task at hand. Any man who knows where he is going is bound to be focused. It ensures that the inevitable distractions will not derail your goals. Successful mountain climbers often set their face like a flint, ready to spark with intensity their inborn passion to take on the challenge in front of them. Goal setting infuses you with energy, as life is boring without direction. When you have found your bearings, your future cannot be easily derailed. Setting a goal for yourself before you take on your mountainous challenge also ensures that you do not carelessly burn your energy on frivolous pursuits. Mountain climbers live a waste-free life because they are committed to the pursuit of their defined goals.

Once you know your purpose in life, it will be evident to you that any mountain that is standing between you and your goals will have to be surmounted. If you do not have a vision about where you are going in life, you will drift from one end of the earth to the other avoiding every mountain and hill on your path, consequently missing out on the thrills and joy of victorious living. You must set goals that enable you to accomplish your highest priority in life.

A victorious mountain climber must prepare to see beyond what their eye can see. When you stand at the foot of a very high mountain, you can barely see the summit with your naked eye. You have to use your inner eye (also called the "eye of the heart") to see yourself at the peak of that mountain celebrating before you ever take the first step. If you don't see yourself at the zenith of the rock, or mountain, you may never get there.

Studies have shown that the most powerful tool for increasing motivation may be visualization. Peak performers, in both business and sports, have shown that they all share one common trait – the ability to visualize the end result of their labor long before it comes to fruition. [3] Most Olympic athletes who visualize themselves on a podium receiving a medal most often do so!

Imagination is not only impacted by what we see but also by what we hear. In fact, more often than not, what you hear affects what you see because the ear is the gateway to the heart and the mind. You have to consciously choose what you hear and whom you choose to communicate with about your aspirations. Not everyone deserves access to your imagination and your spirit.

Before my friend goes on his rock climbing trip, around the clock, he often plays uplifting music on his gadgets, like an MP3 or iPod, that evoke determination and confidence. This is the main reason why you see so many athletes before a big race or sporting event with headphones on listening to music on their MP3s or iPods, especially if they are competing at an arena away from their home stadium. They very often use this music device to tune out the hostile catcalls and intimidation from the opposing fans. What a good reminder that we must be prepared to shut our ears to the naysayers. These are the people who will try to talk you out of facing your challenges.

Often when I ask my rock climbing buddy where he is going next, he tells me about the joy of standing on top of the rock and the pain and grueling hardship he is about to endure. He will often call me into his office to share pictures of the mountains/rocks he had conquered in the past. And then, he will show me the picture of the apex of the current rock he plans to ascend. Frequently, he imagines himself standing victoriously at the top. This is one way he motivates himself for the task ahead.

Successful climbers are motivated by causes, personal or national. Human beings are often motivated by benefit and/or reward. The first inquiry David made before his epic encounter with Goliath was about the benefit that would accrue to whomever was victorious over Goliath. When he heard that this person would get tax exemptions as well as the hand of the king's daughter in marriage, he prepared himself for the challenge. When his brothers asked him what he was doing on the battlefront, his retort was curt and pointed, "Is there not a cause? (I Samuel 17:29b) A cause is a reason or rationale for doing something. There must be a reason for your life. There must be a cause. For many of us facing life's mountainous challenges, it can be so daunting that we soon forget or neglect the inevitable joy that lies ahead. We too quickly forget the cause(s) that drove us to the mountain. Instead of weighing us down, we can use it as a springboard to our destiny. David's personal desire to better his lot in life, at that moment united with a greater cause, which was to defend his homeland from the invading Philistine army. He seized the opportunity. If we are to make our mark in this world, then our desire must be to make our lives count for something. David was not only committed to this worthy cause, but he was willing to give his life to defend it. We have to remind ourselves that our Lord Jesus Christ, the author and finisher of our faith, endured the pain, shame and agony of the cross with the help of the joy that was set before Him. (Hebrews 12:2) When I first arrived in the United States, I had to work as a security guard to support my family. At one of the outposts where the security company sent me, I met a lady who knew me as a successful attorney in Nigeria. At first, she was stunned to see me in a security guard uniform because of my more elevated employment status in my home country. She suddenly burst into derisive laughter while pointing at me and telling everyone around her about me. The lady remarked that America had leveled the playing field and she was now my boss, whereas in Nigeria, she would have been serving me.

All this happened while I was standing a few feet from her. While she tried to humiliate me, in my heart I knew that this was not the end of the story. I walked away at the end of the shift with greater determination and a prayer that my career would not end with me as a security guard in America. Within months of that encounter, I passed my bar exam and resumed my law career but she remained working at the same minimum wage job.

On another occasion, I met a Nigerian cab driver in Washington DC, who upon seeing me in a security guard uniform started cursing me and Nigeria as a country. He never gave me an opportunity to explain myself. None of these people could see beyond my temporary status as a security guard and they really did not want to listen to me. If either of them had cared enough to ask me, I would have enlightened them about where I was going, but they did not care. They saw a guy with great promise working below the level where they imagined I should be. They could not see past my present situation to my future.

What they did not know was that I was patrolling the streets of Southeast DC as a security guard during the night, while I studied for my bar exam in the early morning hours. I enrolled and passed the bar on my very first attempt because I was determined to change my status with the help of God. I would often pray and fast while I read and prepared for the Washington State Bar Exam. Even when I was wearing a security guard uniform, I saw myself appearing before judges and jurors arguing my client's case. My dream in the end came to pass. The mountain they could not imagine I could surmount, I conquered with panache!

> *"When you have vision, it affects your attitude. Your attitude is optimistic rather than pessimistic."*
> *— Charles R. Swindoll*

It is, however, important to emphasize that a determined climber must be ready to know all there is to know about the challenges before him or her. What you know will help you maintain your confidence when everyone is falling down the cliff. The search for knowledge should always start with an assessment of your resources. When you take stock of what you have, you can figure out what you need.

David knew what he had was mightier than the mountain called Goliath. He had the captain of the army of Israel as commander-in-chief. More importantly, he knew the weapon in his hand, the stone in his sling, could reach Goliath faster and cover a greater distance than the speed at which Goliath's spear could reach him. David also knew the enemy. He knew Goliath was skilled in close physical contact, what we call "man o man o" – man to man combat, hence Goliath's call to Israel to appoint someone to fight him. You will never conquer your enemy if you play the game on your enemy's turf. I have seen many Christians fall flat on their face when they thought they knew enough of the Bible to be able to go back to their old friends and old neighborhood where they used to do drugs and still remain clean and sober. It rarely ends well. This is crucial and important because sometimes the challenges we think are "Goliath-like hydra-headed mountains" are mere molehills but for the lack of knowledge. The worst captivity is that of the mind.

My rock climbing friend is often surprised to find out that some mountains and rocks touted online as impossible to climb are often the easiest. Knowledge is the reservoir of strength and confidence you rely upon when you see many of your friends turning back from the mountain base because they are too scared to climb the mountain.

Many of my learned colleagues who were successful lawyers in Nigeria before immigrating to the United States often end up abandoning their practice and the profession. They talk themselves out of it. One who was a close friend could not imagine himself appearing before American jurors with his accent. He said to me, "I don't stand a chance. You are Black and you don't speak like an American. You might as well toss your bar license into the garbage, if you ever pass the bar exam." It was such a joy when I called him after winning my first jury trial. Never allow the negative opinion of your peers to impact your divine assignment.

There are generally two groups of Christians on planet Earth: those who end their race at the foot of the mountain and those who overcome and go beyond their present mountain to greater challenges in the future. The first group of people tend to stop dead in their tracks when they meet a crisis on the first local relief. They dwell on their crisis all day long and massage the crisis and talk about the problems as if they are bigger than their God. The second group finds something useful to hold onto and presses on when they reach a dark steep incline. The greatest strength of overcomers is their reliance on the grace of God.

Very often our first instinct is to confront problems and crisis with all we have and when we fall flat on our face, we get frustrated, angry and disappointed. Writing about climbers who died on Mount Everest, Stewart Green, states, "An analysis of the 212 deaths that happened during the 86-year period from 1921 to 2006 indicates some interesting facts. Most deaths – 192 – occurred above Base Camp, where the technical climbing begins." [4]

Whether the mountainous crisis relates to health, relationships, shelter, career, food or emotional loss, we all tend to focus on our own energy first, and once we run out of steam and are spent, then we start dialing back. It is at this time those who do know God begin to do mighty exploits for Christ.

Rather than dwell on nabobs of negativity, what we ought to do is seek knowledge that will advance our journey. This is because what you know will be of great help when you face the impossible. There are many folks suffering in the world today with the solutions to their nightmares staring them right in the face but they don't recognize it. There are some that think they know what ails them but are easily deceived by shadows. Some know the truth and yet speak lies.

One of the most potent weapons in conquering your mountains is your mouth. No wonder Jesus Christ said "whoever shall say to this mountain" will see it moved and be cast into the sea. Life and death are in the power of the tongue.

What you say about your condition goes a long way in determining whether you get victory over it or not. Later in this book, we shall see how we can build some spiritual muscle of faith through the power of our confession. The Bible tells us that what Job knew and said, helped him face the disasters in his life. (Job 12&13) It helped him confront his friends who wanted him to deny God. Job told his friends you can't intimidate me, I am not inferior to you. He said, "I know I shall be justified…for I know that my redeemer lives!" Finally, he knew that God can do anything. (Job 13:18; 19:25; 42:2) This is the confession of someone that knows whom he believes in. Those who know their God shall be strong and do mighty exploits. Don't ever underestimate the power of what you know. Today start studying the Word of God and speaking the truth that you find.

An essential part of knowledge is an understanding of what you have. Assess all the tools you have in your arsenal to take on your mountain climb. Sometimes we are easily overwhelmed by the sheer might of the enemy and what we know about the opponent. This is the bane of many Christians today. We develop an inferiority complex, all of which is mainly due to our ignorance of the God we serve and our own lack of understanding of who we are in God.

Some denominations are set up to study and understand the devil. They pray, fast and do an in-depth study of the devil and demonology neglecting the study of Christ, who gives us the power to overcome. Hence, they have little or no knowledge of God's promise of victory in all things. They know a lot about the devil but very little about the God who promised that above all we are more than conquerors. (Romans 8:37)

We learn a unique story about the power of knowledge from the Bible in II Chronicles 13:1-10. It is the story of King Abijah of Judah, who when confronted by Jeroboam's 800,000 mighty men of valor army, rallied his troops which were about half the size of the opponent's army, by a unique application of knowledge, courage and faith.

First of all, he personally climbed Mount Zemaraim, which is in Mount Ephraim. He then stood on top of the mountain to address the people. There is no doubt that it takes a lot of courage to stand on top of a mountain in the midst of the battle. You become an easy target, easily spotted by the enemy and vulnerable to attack. King Abijah knew this was the best way to motivate his frightened army. If they could see he was not afraid, he knew they would go with him.

I don't know if you are the CEO of a troubled company or a pastor at a local church about to be foreclosed upon by the bank, but what you need to do is lead the people of God by standing on top of the "mountain of vulnerability". Mountain climbers are courageous leaders. When you make yourself vulnerable by being open and transparent with the people you lead and do it with confidence and panache, then you will in turn infuse your followers with a strong belief that the battle can be won.

Next, he reminded everyone what he knew about the Word of God. He knew the God factor, meaning that he knew God was the source of his claim to the throne. He challenged them to remember that the Lord God of Israel gave the kingdom to his great grandfather, David, by a covenant of salt. The Bible says the children of Judah prevailed "because they relied upon the Lord God of their fathers." (II Chronicles 13:18)

I ask again, what do you know about your God? What do you know about yourself? What do you know about your enemy? What do you know about the mountain before you? Knowledge is good, but what we do with the knowledge gained is of more importance. Someone once said wisdom is the application of knowledge obtained. For instance, hikers are usually cautioned to avoid steep spring snow in the afternoon after the sun warms it.

Mark Obmascik writes about the story of Brian Smith, a fifty-four year old hiker from Santa Monica, California who while hiking unprepared through a snowy scramble across Kelso Ridge of Torreys Peak in Colorado, at 3:40 p.m. "crunched through a snow cornice and cartwheeled down the appropriately named Dead Dog Couloir. Rescue crews figured he fell more than a thousand feet, or about the height of the Eiffel Tower." [5]

What you know will determine your promotion and elevation if you put it to good use. After all, what good is a lesson learned if it is not put to good use?

Divine secrets are priceless assets on our life's journey. Every star in the Bible was forged out of access to the deep secrets of the Divine. Daniel goes boldly to the king and proclaims "there is a God in heaven that reveals secrets." Daniel was promoted once he knew the dream and its interpretation with the help of God. It is only in God's presence that you will obtain the knowledge that will enable you to overcome your mountain. Psalm 25:14 says that "the secret of the Lord is with them who fear Him and He will show them His covenant." (KJV) Joseph, who interpreted another king's dream, said to his brothers in Genesis 42:18, "This do, and live, for I fear God."(KJV)

> *"Vision without execution is hallucination."*
> — Thomas Edison

There is a sad story in the Bible about knowledge and the elongation of slavery. In Genesis 15:13, the Lord said unto Abram that surely his seed would be a stranger in a land that was not theirs and shall serve and be afflicted four hundred years. We, however, find that in actual fact the children of Israel were in slavery in Egypt for four hundred and thirty years! What gives? Did God lie? Was Abram deceived? We know for a fact that God cannot lie, because He is not a man that He should lie and neither the son of man that He should repent. (Numbers 23:19) We find the key to understanding exactly what happened in Acts 7:22-25.

The Bible says, Moses thought the children of Israel should have known that God by His hand would deliver them but they did not understood. They did not know! They extended their own slavery by thirty years out of ignorance! Here is where it gets really sad. Those extra thirty years were the most difficult because it was during the reign of a Pharaoh that did not know Joseph. In fact, he was the cruelest ruler that ever graced the throne of Egypt. They were oppressed like never before, they worked without pay. It was the most austere time of their lives.

Sometimes we get carried away by the "sugar rush" and the thrill of mountaineering, forgetting that the path to the mountaintop is strewn with the carcasses and debris of those who are not prepared for the inclement weather mid-rift. Writing on the causes of fatalities on Mount Everest, Stewart Green again opines, as follows, "The mortality rate was 1.3 percent, with the rate for climbers (mostly non-natives) at 1.6 percent and the rate for Sherpas, natives of the region and usually acclimatized to high elevations, at 1.1 percent. The annual death rate is remarkably unchanged over the history of climbing on Mount Everest. One death occurs for every ten successful ascents – a significant number of climbers who reach the summit die on their descent. Most climbers who die on Everest are generally physically fit and in the prime of their life between the ages of 30 and 50." [6]

Our first concern should not always be the rush to the top but an understanding of the process that will get us there. God sees our difficulties, He even said, "Be still and know that I am God." (Psalm 46:10) It is only those who take a breather, meditate deep and know that He is God that will realize that God is highly exalted above their mountainous problems. He sees our path better than we do because He is above us all. The dangerous path is laced with thorns, and the easy path leads to victory.

Knowledge of God will reveal to us that God is more interested in getting us "over" the mountain than off the mountain. I once crawled to church because of searing back pain. When I got to church, I could barely stand to worship, and as we were singing, a word of knowledge came through me that God was healing those with bad backs and I didn't even know I was talking about myself. After the word, I checked my back and found no searing pain. I was ecstatic!

Knowledge and information are crucial to success in any modern sport, even more so in mountain or rock climbing. A lot of people perish on the molehill of ignorance. They get lost trying to find the starting point of their climb. Some even end up climbing mountains that are not meant for them and will not yield them any appreciable reward. To avoid climbing up to a dead end, arrived at by trial and error as well as misinformation, you need to be well equipped with knowledge and understanding of the challenges before you. Heed good advice from those who know more than you. Accept their offer to help, as we don't know it all. Mark Obmascik writes of an eighty-seven year old woman who was too stubborn to accept a car ride home from the top of Pikes Peak in Colorado and "insisted on hiking back down the mountain by herself despite an approaching storm; her body was found eleven days later." [7]

Know your source, assess what you have, understand the challenges before you and speak life into your situation. The first thing David inquired about before taking on the Goliath challenge was the reward that awaited Goliath's conqueror. They told him such a person would be tax free as well as get the king's beautiful daughter. He immediately stepped up to the plate.

Confident, positive climbers are highly motivated successful climbers.[8] If all you confess is negativity, the chances of you ever climbing above the world's lowest sea level is greatly reduced. The Bible says as a man thinks in his heart, so is he. (Proverbs 23:7) And a good man out of the good treasure of his heart brings forth good. (Luke 6:45) You must be aware of your negative thoughts and learn to counter such thoughts with positive uplifting confessions. Imagine 17 year old David, in I Samuel 17, telling his country's president (King Saul) in the presence of his highest ranking military commanders, "let no man's heart fail because of him; your servant will go and fight with this Philistine." (I Samuel 17:32) This is an audacious and infectious courage. If you want to be significant in life, you need infectious courage. The world is full of fearful cowards looking for inspiration from the children of God. A day-to-day effort to turn your negative thoughts around can have a dramatic effect on your confidence and the motivation to face your challenges.

Why is this important? By speaking to every crag, talus, difficult mountain cliff or "local relief" on our way to the peak of the mountain, this exercise of faith helps release an abundance of courage and strength in our time of need. It is a lot easier to move the entire mountain so you don't have to climb it! But what exactly does God wants you to do in this circumstance? That should be the first place we start. Pray. Seek His face. You may be as surprised as the prophet Habakkuk who found out in his prayer (Habakkuk 3) that all you need to do is rejoice and not curse the enemy or pray for revenge. (Habakkuk 3:16-19) (NLT) Practice sitting back, closing your eyes, praising God and visualizing yourself at the zenith of your mountains. In essence, the right approach to our besetting challenges should be drawn from the leading of the Holy Spirit and not a perfunctory decision based on an emotional roller coaster. Even when the flocks die and the cattle barns are empty, yet, I will rejoice in the Lord. (Habakkuk 3:17-18) (NLT) Find out the mind of God as touching your circumstances and follow His leading. As you praise Him and rejoice, He will make your path straight. He will guide you into His knowledge.

Lack of knowledge about the challenges before you, not only slows your progress it may eventually leave you frustrated and dejected until you find your bearings again through knowledge. People don't necessarily fail an exam because they know nothing. Very often people fail exams because what they know is not enough! What you know determines where you are now, because if you knew the easy route to the peak of your mountain you would have taken it. Prayer is not a substitute for knowledge. It is the answer you get from knowing the One who answers our prayers. You need to find your way to your source.

In climbing your mountainous challenges, you need a guidebook, a line of fixed gear or a chalk to follow. [9] There is no better guidebook than the manual of life. "All scripture," the Bible says, "is given by inspiration of God and is profitable for doctrine, for reproof, for correction, for instruction in righteousness that the man of God may be complete, thoroughly equipped for every good work." (II Timothy 3:16-17)

I am convinced any inquiries about your vision should start with your manufacturer's manual. Your manual is your Source's written word for you and it is meant to guide and encourage you. All computer software begins with a written code or programming scripting or coding. The purpose of programming is to create a set of instructions that the computer uses to perform specific operations or to exhibit desired behaviors. The process of writing source code for computer software often requires expertise in many different subjects including knowledge of the application domain, specialized algorithms and formal logic.

> *"It is very dangerous to go into eternity with possibilities which one has oneself prevented from becoming realities. A possibility is a hint from God. One must follow it."— Sören Kierkegaard*

Your Creator had a specific purpose in mind when He created you and He wrote a specific set of instructions so you can exhibit desired behaviors. When software malfunctions, very often someone or malware (the devil, sin, cares of this world) has tampered with the source code. To return back to the original source, you have to go back to your manufacturer's source code (the Bible) to find your specific domain (where He meant for you to be), your algorithms (the process and steps He has prepared for you to function adequately) and your formal logic (your thoughts/choices). He is the only one that knows what ails you and He will never keep you in the dark.

The vision for your life is a secret hidden in the heart of God, your Source and your Maker, and He is willing to reveal it to you. Your psychologist may not know what is wrong with you or where you are going. In fact, your medical doctor may have written you off as terminal. But as one of my rock climbing buddies once intoned, "We are all terminal with an attitude." The reason why all the professional examiners may not know what ails you, may have little or nothing to do with their qualifications, because the Word of God says "...eye hath not seen, nor ear heard, neither have entered into the heart of man, the things which God hath prepared for them that love him." The passage goes on to assure us, "But God hath revealed them unto us by his Spirit; for the Spirit searcheth all things, yea, even the deep things of God." (I Corinthians 2:9-10) (KJV)

Discovering our vision and potential is also directly linked to our endowment. Everyone is endowed by their maker with specific talents and gifts. The discovery of your passion and talents is a veritable avenue for locating your purpose in life. The major difference between Spirit-inspired vision and purpose derived from our endowed ability is the dichotomy between divine discovery and self-discovery. To succeed at the latter, your gift will have to make room for you whereas success at the former is totally by the grace of the Divine or by waiting on the Spirit.

Your vision may be revealed to you in your dreams. A woman of God once had a dream to start an Easter drama with the details of the scenes revealed to her in that dream. She woke up to discover the mountains standing between her and her dream were many. One by one, she took them on, issues of location, cast members, funding, publicity, et cetera. Today that dream has become such a huge reality that it is now one of the largest Christian gatherings in the Inland Northwest of the United States of America – Spokane Dream Center's "Behold Jesus" Easter Drama.

Your vision needs to be written down and kept because you will get to a point in your journey, on the way to the top, where you will need to pull it out and use it to encourage you. The woman of God I mentioned in the preceding paragraph – Pastor Alice Darroch, when she faced challenges along the way, had to refer to her dream about the Easter drama. She and her husband wrote a book about their journey as they conquered their mountains. [10] More often than not, your vision will be bigger than you. The assurance that you are pursuing a vision higher than yourself is such that it would necessarily fuel your passion and keep you going during times of hardship and suffering when it looks like the mountain is too high for you.

But vision in and of itself can only carry you so far. You need to be prepared in more ways than one. The best preparation for a successful mountain conquest is to climb, climb and climb some more. A lot of people wait at the foot of Mount Everest gazing at it, overwhelmed by its sheer height even though they have never summoned the courage to climb the hillside in their hometown. In the Book of Job, we learn that there are some whose beginnings are small and insignificant but their latter end will increase greatly. (Job 8:7)

When I first immigrated to the United States, I had been a lawyer in Nigeria for more than seven years. Working in one of the top law firms in Nigeria, I left behind a lot of opportunities because I was convinced that the United States would be a better fit for my career given the political problems in my country at the time. Upon my arrival, I discovered I couldn't just walk in and begin practicing law. Only a few states allowed legal practitioners from common law countries to sit for their bar exams when they had not attended an American law school. I had a family to support and I couldn't afford to stand around dependent on welfare forever. So I applied to take the bar exam in the state of Washington, while I worked as a security guard in Washington DC. I knew I had to find a way to practice law in any capacity so as to continue to stoke my passion for the profession.

One day I walked into a legal publishing company and informed them that I was volunteering to work in their library for free. At first they thought I was joking. I asked them to take me to their library and I would show them what I intended to do. They did and within minutes I pointed out several things that needed to be done to make their workplace a lot better. The manager embraced my ideas and informed the owner who opened the door for this opportunity. They could not believe I was willing to work for free.

What they did not understand was that I needed them more than they needed me. I needed a place to fan the embers of my interest in law while I waited to take the bar exam. I needed to familiarize myself with the American workplace and law reports. My volunteer work with this firm was a bountiful blessing to me and to them. They were so enamored with some of the innovative changes I made to their library that they threw a wonderful party for me after I passed my bar exam and was ready to leave the DC area.

More importantly, however, is the fact that I never saw myself as working for more than six months as a volunteer librarian. I never doubted my desire to practice law in the United States. But if I had not taken that job as a stopgap measure, I may never have realized my dream. What is more, that job prepared me for the American work environment which is quite different and distinct from the laid-back working environment I was used to in Nigeria.

My schedule included making telephone calls to the security headquarters office, interacting with clients and other duties. I also used this time of waiting to register for computer training during the day, as I had never worked on a computer in Nigeria.

To pay for the class, I had to take out a student loan of $6,000 which I paid off from my minimum wage job as a security guard. In the meantime, my payments to Sallie Mae helped improve my credit history so much so that when I applied to buy my first house, my banker had no problem with my credit history. This is not an indictment on those who have to survive on a welfare check. My wife and I probably took advantage of one or two government welfare programs during those lean years of our lives and I have no regret for doing so. Indeed, there are many who need the assistance and the relief this program brings.

There are those who started out on the welfare rolls and are today owners of their own Fortune 500 companies. The important thing is never to detest the day of small beginnings. Don't stand on the foothills of the future when today's little challenges could easily give you a leg up that you can use to surmount tomorrow's mountains. The journey of a thousand miles starts with the first step; it is time to begin your journey to the peak of your destiny. Arise.

PRINCIPLES

1. Successful mountain climbers put a lot of effort into preparation.

2. Proper preparation prevents poor performance.

3. Failure in life is not necessarily due to a lack of opportunity, but a lack of preparation.

4. You can control how prepared you are but you can't control most of your opportunities.

5. A call or summons from someone at the top of the mountain is not necessarily a command to go up immediately, it is often a signal to prepare yourself to go up.

6. David was anointed by Samuel in Bethlehem, not to ascend the throne immediately, but to prepare himself for the task ahead.

7. The big difference between the failure of King Saul and the success of King David is preparation.

8. Preparation starts with vision. Aspire to become something bigger than your mountain.

9. Preparation also starts with goal setting. Goal setting helps you focus on the task at hand.

10. Imagination is not only impacted by what we see but also by what we hear.

11. Human beings are often motivated by benefit and/or reward.

12. What you know will help maintain your confidence when everyone is falling down the cliff.

13. The worst captivity is that of the mind.

14. Knowledge is the reservoir of strength and confidence you rely upon when you see many of your friends turning back to the lowlands from the mountain base because they are too scared to climb the mountain.

15. There are generally two groups of Christians on planet Earth: those who end their race at the foot of the mountain and those who overcome and go beyond their present mountain to greater challenges in the future.

16. One of the most potent weapons in conquering your mountains is your mouth.

17. An essential part of knowledge is an understanding of what you have.

18. Assess all the tools you have in your arsenal to take on your mountain climb.

19. Divine secrets are priceless assets on our life's journey.

20. Every star in the Bible was forged out of access to the deep secrets of the Divine.

21. Knowledge of God will reveal to us that God is more interested in getting us "over" the mountain than off the mountain.

22. Know your source, assess what you have, understand the challenges before you and speak life into your situation.

23. In climbing your mountainous challenges, you need a guidebook, a line of fixed gear or a chalk to follow.

24. Discovering our vision and potential is also directly linked to our endowment.

25. The best preparation for a successful mountain conquest is to climb, climb and climb some more.

26. Don't stand on the foothills of the future when today's little challenges could easily give you a leg up that you can use to surmount tomorrow's mountains.

27. It is time to begin your journey to the peak of your destiny. Arise.

DISCUSSION GUIDE

1. What are the things the Lord has been preparing you for?

2. Write out your vision for your marriage, family and organization.

3. Write out what you are doing now that aligns with your dream.

4. Itemize the things you are doing now that are not in any way connected to your dream.

5. What motivates you? Money? Fame? Discuss with your group the different sources of motivation in our society today. Evaluate them using God's standard, the Bible, to determine if they align with the Word of God.

CHAPTER SIX
PACK YOUR BACKPACK, LEAVE YOUR BAGGAGE: GEAR VS. THE ELEMENTS

A twenty-six year old man once defied the National Park Service's warnings about icy conditions and climbed Longs Peak in September in jeans, tennis shoes, and a cotton hoodie; he died of hypothermia on the summit when a snowstorm blew in. ...The vast majority of victims, however, were not ones who ignored obvious warning signs ...
–Mark Obsmascik [1]

Mountain climbing is not a stroll down the street. If this were so, then many people would be at their peak when they face mountainous problems. It is also not a walk in the park. You need more than just the will to climb a mountain to reach the summit. This is because as Brandon Mathis, writing about the very physical sport of mountaineering pointed out, "Mountain climbing is a gear-intensive activity. Whether you plan to ascend a sheer cliff wall or tackle a multi-day expedition in the Himalayas, bringing the right gear is essential." [2] There is no doubt that the same principle applies to both figurative and physical mountains. Without the necessary tools, hardware and gear, one can easily be blown away by inclement weather and unsalutary climbing environments. Appropriate gear is necessary whether you are negotiating a sheer cliff, a local relief, steep or gentle ascent, rocky ground or slippery ice.

Appropriate gear connotes the essentials. This is not a journey where you can check in your luggage at the airport and have a carryon with you. In fact, the bare essentials are all you need for mountain or rock climbing, don't bring your luggage. You have to learn to trust that God will provide for your needs if He asks you to climb any mountain in life. Trusting Him for your provisions is crucial. This explains the prophet Habakkuk's earnest prayer: "The Sovereign Lord is my strength! He will make me as surefooted as a deer and bring me safely over the mountain." (Habakkuk 3:19) (NLT) This is the cry of a man who is neither taking his mountainous challenge lightly nor deluded by any self-belief. He realizes that if he is to make it safely over the mountain of life, he has to be totally dependent on God's sovereign strength which will make him surefooted like a deer and then bring him safely to the summit. Throughout this process the prophet is not deluded into thinking that he will make it successfully over the mountain by his own power and strength.

In life, many people are marching up the hills with all sorts of baggage, both physical and emotional. Some are in a relationship they are not meant to be in but are trying to plod along so as to prove a point or not let down their parents. They have what they call "self-belief" – something which is finite. Others have nothing near their self-belief and yet keep plodding on, so they get jealous, bitter and envious. The guy with limited self-belief will often rely on God's everlasting arms, while the guy with "macho" self-belief is too arrogant to ask for help.

A person who carries emotional baggage through life is not going to go far on the journey to the mountaintop. There are bags full of your conscious and unconscious mistakes. Some bags are stuffed with things that have been done to you while others contain other people's opinions about you that still control your life, seven or twenty years after the fact. You haven't forgiven yourself or let them go.

All this baggage defines you in a negative way. Some people's bags are stuffed full to the brim with unresolved issues, offenses, unforgiveness, anger, bitterness or hatred. This baggage gets harder and harder to lug up the mountain as you ascend higher and higher. You may need to throw away this excess baggage to get in shape. Even the luggage that is essential should not be on your shoulders, it is time to put it on the shoulders of the one whom the government of the world rests upon.

Emotional baggage only hurts you. The people you are refusing to forgive may have already moved on. This baggage of hurt, bitterness, jealousy and pain cuts across cultures, peoples and individuals even though not all of us carry the same amount of baggage.

The first question to ask yourself is, what do you have in your house/ backpack? That was the question the Man of God asked the heavily indebted widow who went to Elisha begging for assistance to pay her debt so her son would not be sold into slavery. Many people in life do not believe they have anything of worth that can be used to produce their miracle. Too many people are waiting for God to heal their Lazarus as well as roll the stone away. Jesus asked those around him to roll the stone away from the tomb once He asked Lazarus to come forth.

The heavily indebted widow helped by Elisha was facing a domestic and financial nightmare. Her children were facing slavery because of a debt incurred in the lifetime of her husband, who was one of the sons of the prophet. It seemed that she had nothing to offer and yet Elisha asked her two questions, what can I do for you? And, what do you have in your house?

The first question placed responsibility for performance on Elisha whereas the second question put the onus on the woman. She chose to answer the second question. The question you choose to respond to very often determines the quality of the answer you will receive and the mountains you conquer. [3] She said, "I have nothing but a jar of oil." Elisha then used that jar of oil to help her get her miracle.

Many today are standing at the foot of their mountain looking for a miracle that will suddenly take them to the summit, when all they need to start the climb is already in their backpack. Many do not know that God will not do for you, what you can do for yourself. We should not deny the fact that some have the odds stacked against them, both deserved and undeserved. Some by accidents of birth, others due to their own choices are paying the price. No matter the odds stacked against you, you still have a chance to improve your situation.

The Bible tells the story of a blind man, called Bartimaeus, son of Timaeus, everything imaginable was lined up against this man. He was blind and was known for his blindness. Bartimaeus heard Jesus was passing by but he was surrounded by crowds of people. He had no way of making it successfully through the crowd to Jesus. He was physically challenged as a result of his blindness even though he was born with a good last name. The crowd surrounding Jesus was not friendly to him. They

A person who carries emotional baggage through life is not going to go far on the journey to the mountaintop.

outshouted him, telling him to keep quiet when he tried to get Jesus' attention. Blind Bartimaeus did not stand a chance in this situation. The odds indeed were stacked against him. The likelihood he could conquer the insurmountable problem of blindness was greatly decreased by the unfriendly crowd.

Many people have been hurt by the crowd, even by the church people who hang around Jesus. These are the people who throng around the altar and hug the pulpit. They tell outsiders like Bartimaeus they own the Jesus trademark. It would be easy for Bartimaeus to hang on to these facts as an excuse to remain at the foot of his mountain, but he did not.

There is a brother of mine who sees everything in this world in a negative light. When he sees men and women of God, he does not see people who can pray for him but people fleecing the flock. It doesn't matter if all the reasons he has for such conclusions are mere rumors and innuendoes. Blind Bartimaeus, on the other hand, did not allow those who hung around Jesus to hinder his desire to have his sight restored so he could overcome his mountain.

He looked into his backpack determined to overcome his limitations and reached deep inside to find the only thing he had to eliminate his mountainous problem and he found – his voice. Blindness may have taken his eyes, his good name and the ability to mingle with the crowd but it hadn't taken his voice.

Like Bartimaeus, there is something left in your backpack to sustain your mountain climb – reach for it right now. Bartimaeus knew his voice was the only thing left and he was not going to allow anyone to take that from him by silencing him. The Bible says he cried out saying, "Jesus, Son of David, have mercy on me." (Mark 10:47) He knew instinctively that today was his day, it was the day his preparation met his opportunity. Bartimaeus knew he had to use what he had, to get what he wanted. He was desperate and hungry to surmount his mountain. Sometimes you need an attitude of desperation to get beyond your limitations. He was not willing to take no for an answer that day.

Today, millions of people in the world are looking for something they have lost, a search which brings heartache and pain that often ends in frustration. They often forget that the principal thing needed for such a search is in their hands. Stop crying over spilt milk and start your search in the right direction by appreciating what you have, because what you have will point you in the right direction to find what you have lost.

Bartimaeus had no eyesight and was desperate to see. All he had left was his voice, so he used his voice to get his eyes restored. What do you have in your backpack? Search deep and find what will get you to the peak of your mountain. My friend is very meticulous in packing his backpack for his rock climbing trip. He takes everything out and takes an inventory to ensure he has the supplies necessary for the trip.

Let's examine some of the equipment necessary for a successful rock or mountain climb. Brandon Mathis, a mountaineering enthusiast and blogger for Livestrong.org writes this about the importance of having the right garment for climbing. "Often in the mountains the day may look clear only to give way to furious weather of high winds, rain and snow, followed by an afternoon of sunshine. Being prepared with proper clothing like a jacket/shell and pant that resists weather is your best defense to stay comfortable and safe in a mountain environment…Like hardware and protective equipment, clothing is an essential part of the mountain climber's gear." [4]

Just as technology has impacted our daily grind, it has also helped mountaineers and rock climbers navigate the besetting daily problems of a tough climb. The boom in backpacking accessories is all over the internet and every retail outfit. Modern equipment helps enthusiasts and mountaineer sports competitors go a long way up the cliff with little or no break in between. The climbs that used to take ages are now easily summited by thousands seeking the glorious view at the apex with the most beautiful landscapes.

The sad thing, however, is that some equipment, vitamins and gear are made to enable users to cut corners, but at great expense to your body and mind. All of which makes the reliability of old tried and tested equipment more valuable than ever. No wonder Paul speaking of the believer's most necessary apparel strongly urges us to "put on the whole armor of God that you may be able to stand against the wiles of the devil." (Ephesians 6:11)

Paul went on to lay bare the essential hardware and protective equipment needed for believers and he starts with the belt of truth. When I asked a group of mountain climbing enthusiasts what is the most important gear needed for a successful mountain climbing experience, they all chorused "harness". A harness is what wraps around your waist and legs and attaches to climbing and rappelling ropes for safety, protection, comfort and ease. The harness binds you for safety. The word "harness" in Hebrew is "qal" or "acar" which means to bind, or join together, saddle or govern.

We have stated that every journey to the summit must start with a Word from God. You can't embark on a journey and be successful without the leading of the Lord. The Word of the Lord you receive is what will keep you going on the day of need. The interesting thing here is that the belt of truth is what Paul first talked about when addressing the whole armor of God that every believer needs to put on. (Ephesians 6:14)

Why is this important? Because we do not wrestle against flesh and blood but against powers and principalities. It is also the Word of the Lord that you receive before embarking on the journey that will sustain you in every dry spell along the way. The Word of the Lord protects you and is also a divine compass on the confusing steeps and slopes of the mountains of life.

For instance, after delivering the children of Israel from slavery in Egypt, God gave them stern warnings repeatedly to bind His Word upon their hands and as frontlets between their eyes. (Deuteronomy 6:8, 11:18; Exodus 13:16) Every time they honor the Word of God, they prosper and easily overcome every difficult mountain on their path. But when they neglect the Word of the Lord they fall into the hand of the enemy. In fact, in one instance, the prophet Micaiah, successfully predicted their fall when they served other gods, "And he said, I saw all Israel scattered upon the hills, as sheep that have not a shepherd." (I Kings 22:17)(KJV)

The protection afforded by the harness helps keep you from drifting away or getting lost on the cliffs as you climb. Here is His assurance, "I will seek that which was lost, and bring again that which was driven away, and will bind up that which was broken, and will strengthen that which was sick." (Ezekiel 34:16)(KJV) The Lord knows there will be moments when you get tired or drift off to sleep as you climb, or even when you get sick.

Stewart Green writing about the major causes of death on Everest said, "Along with extreme fatigue, many Everest climbers who die develop symptoms like loss of coordination, confusion, lack of judgment, and they may even slip into unconscious (sic) – all symptoms of high-altitude cerebral edema (HACE). HACE often occurs at high elevations when the brain swells from the leakage of cerebral blood vessels." [5]

The Word of God assures us that He will bind you with the harness of His Word so He can find you when you are lost or driven away by the enemy. (Hosea 6:1-2) The cool thing is when He finds you, He will bind every brokenness in you. (Isaiah 61:1) When you get to a point where you bruise yourself on the scraggy cleft of the rock of life, He said, through His harness He will heal your physical and emotional wounds including depression. (Psalm 147:3)

Here is the awesome thing about that. Jesus put His guarantee and warranty on it, when He said, "Whatever you bind on earth will be bound in heaven." (Matthew 18:18) That should give you a reason to reach for the Word of God right now as you prepare to climb or if you are at a point of tiredness and fatigue as you climb up the mountain. So how important is the harness to a successful spiritual mountaineer? The Bible says it is the Father's command that must be treasured and kept secure so we don't falter. (Proverbs 6:21; 7:1-2)

What are these words? We find them in the same passage, "Hear, O Israel: The Lord our God, the Lord is one! You shall love the Lord your God with all your heart, with all your soul, and with all your strength. And these words which I command you today shall be in your heart." (Deuteronomy 6:4-6) When you love God, you are bound to obey His Word. When you love Him, you are fearless in taking on life's many difficult mountainous challenges. As you know, He will never fail you or disappoint you. The Harness is your love for the Word of God. We must bind them around our neck, write them on the tablet of our hearts and gird our loins with it. (Proverbs 3:3)

You can call it the Word, a rope, or a belt or a sword, all I ask is never leave home without it, especially given the fact that you can deploy it as a sword (Ephesians 6:17) and as a belt. (Ephesians 6:14) I believe the Word of God is the infallible truth of God for man.

Brandon Mathis writing about ten essential items for mountain climbing, said, "Mountain climbing rope is much thicker and more durable than average rope, and is applicable to everything from scaling a cliff side to pulling yourself up a steep, icy ascent. Climbing rope comes in a variety of lengths and widths depending on the type of expedition. Thicker, longer ropes are generally used for rock climbing and rappelling. Thinner rope can be used for less severe climbs that still require assistance along an ascent, such as a steep ice field." [6]

Faith is the bridge that connects us to our invisible expectations.

What Mathis is saying here is that there are ropes and there are ropes. Some ropes are unreliable for mountain climbing. We can also extrapolate that to say there are words and there are words. Faith does not rest on promises but it rests upon the character of the person who makes it. As A. W. Tozer said, a promise is as good as the character of the one who makes it. [7] A man's word is his bond. Some men will tell you it is dawn and knowing their antecedent behavior, you are tempted to step outside and check to be sure.

The good thing about the Word of God is that a promise made is a promise kept. This is because God's promises do not emanate from a hollow spirit. [8] Jesus said whatsoever you shall ask the Father in My name, He will give you. (John 16:23) What makes this promise a rope we can hang on to is not the mere promise itself but the infallible and trustworthy character of God. His word proceeds directly from His character and integrity, and so, He is not limited or constrained by anything or anyone.

If He promises to get you up the hill and the mountain, He will surely keep His word. Hang on to the rope He throws you. He is ever faithful and dependable. He is not a politician or a stock broker. He is neither looking for your vote nor your approval. When He said, "I will never leave you nor forsake you" (Hebrews

13:5b) He meant it and He will perform His Word. His Word is powerful because God is omnipotent.

Aside from God's unfailing promises, the Word of God also does much more. Paul writing to Timothy about the Word of God helps us understand the four dimensions of God's Word: "All scripture is given by inspiration of God, and is profitable for doctrine, for reproof, for correction, for instruction in righteousness. That the man of God may be perfect, thoroughly furnished unto all good works." (II Timothy 3:16-17) (KJV) Just as climbing ropes come in a variety of lengths and widths depending on the type of expedition, the Word of God also has different dimensions.

The first dimension is "doctrine" which is from the Greek word "didaskalia" which can be roughly translated as standard or precept, a basis for the function or the manufacturer's information, the manual for learning and teaching.

The second dimension "reproof" is from the Greek word "elegchos" which again can be translated as incontrovertible direct evidence, an unassailable proof beyond all doubt, a reliable piece of evidence for which a criminal conviction can be made, or accurate and indefatigable solid evidence that has been tested and found solid.

The third dimension "correction" is from the Greek word, "epanorthosis" which means rectification, reconciliation through reformation; restoration back to the right or upright state; correction or improvement of life, character or nature.

The fourth dimension is "instruction" from the Greek feminine noun "paideia" which means to nurture back to health through education and training, prescriptions which increase value, by curbing passion sometimes through chastening or chastisement, to cultivate the soul.

It is evident that whatever your condition might be, whether your mountain climbing is Spirit-driven – God is ready to use his rope of doctrine to guide your path or sin driven – He is ready to reprove and restore your soul with correction and instruction that will get you to the summit He meant for you. Do not despair or in any way be dismayed. He is ready to nurture you and improve your life. Hang on to the rope of His Word! Stand up and get going with the belt fastened and ready for deployment.

Charles H. Spurgeon in a sermon delivered at the Metropolitan Tabernacle, Newington, on April 19, 1891 counseled all believers to stand "our defense and our conquest must be obtained by sheer fighting. Many try compromise; but if you are a true Christian, you can never do this business well." [9]

The next essential element of a successful mountain climber is the helmet. Many mountain climbers wear helmets to protect themselves against a fall, a falling rock or another climber's fall. Brandon Mathis writes that "mountain climbing helmets generally protect the entire head and fasten beneath the chin via a strap with a clip. ... Some mountain climbing helmets include attachments for headlamps." [10]

Spiritually, I am convinced this is a strong metaphor for the protection of the soul. Paul in his epistle to the Ephesians, counsels the New Testament believers to take the helmet of salvation and the sword of the Spirit, which is the Word of God, simultaneously. In other words, don't leave home with one forgetting the other. Don't claim to be saved and then neglect the Word of God nor read the Bible while you deny the power of Christ to save. It is interesting that mountain helmets include attachments for headlamps. Paul said among those we wrestle against are the "rulers of the darkness of this age." (Ephesians 6:12) We therefore need the light of the gospel of Christ to dispel such darkness. Salvation saves us from the corrupting influences of this world and the light of the word of salvation exposes all forms of deception of the devil and "gods of this world".

Jesus is the light of the world and the captain of our salvation. The proper Greek translation of the word "take" used here is to accept or receive the salvation offered by Christ in faith. Matthew Henry writing about the helmet of salvation in his commentary said, "A good hope of salvation, well founded and well built, will both purify the soul and keep it from being defiled by Satan, and it will comfort the soul and keep it from being troubled and tormented by Satan. He would tempt us to despair; but good hope keeps us trusting in God, and rejoicing in him." [11]

When combined with the sword of the Spirit which is the only offensive weapon we have, safety and protection are assured. Modern mountain climbers often carry tweezers or a small knifelike blade which can be used to pull out thorns, stingers and the like. This is comparable to the sword of the spirit which is the Word of God that helps us dislodge anything that the Lord has not planted in our lives. The journey to the summit can be perilous but the Lord assures us that He will not leave us defenseless. He knows what we need and He has made provision for us, it is now up to us to pick it up and use it.

Next is footwear, no mountain climber can successfully negotiate the difficult terrain of a scraggy rock or an icy mountain without appropriate footwear. You can't wear your "show off" shoes to climb. Again we turn to Brandon Mathis for the essential footwear for mountaineers "mountain boots that provide comfort and ankle stability are key." [12]

Paul urges all believers to "shod your feet with the preparation of the gospel of peace." (Ephesians 6:15) The more things change, the more they stay the same. During Paul's time, shoes or greaves of brass were exclusively reserved for soldiers and princes. They were used principally to defend against gall-traps, sharp sticks which enemies often lay to obstruct military advances. Matthew Henry writes that those who fell upon them were labeled as unfit to march and serve. We are to be prepared in season and out of season to preach and spread the gospel of Christ which enables us to walk and climb with a steady pace regardless of the obstacles on the way up to the summit. It is the gospel of peace, peace with God, peace with men and peace with ourselves. I have often informed those who care to ask me that the way to genuine peace in the world is to spread the gospel of Christ.

Sometimes mountain climbs get dangerous, and experienced climbers have to use sound judgment, current information and technical mountain climbing gear to successfully navigate hard and difficult terrain. Some inexperienced climbers give into the impulse to set the fastest climb record at the price of safety and pay dearly for it. Mark Obmascik quoted Ricky Denesik, who broke several speed records in mountain climbing as saying, "What I learned, is that the mountains are very powerful and they don't care how fast I want to climb them." He also quoted Denesik partner, Ricky Trujilo, as having said a truism that now guides record seekers everywhere: "Time is gained not by moving faster, but rather by avoiding mistakes and linking key peaks with traverses." [13] Those who don't heed this truism often pay dearly with their lives.

Brandon Mathis writing about good technical gear said, good climbers "use dynamic, stretchable ropes tied to lead climbers, who must navigate a route up the mountain while placing protective gear in various weaknesses in the rock like cracks or slots." [14] Climbers then clip the rope to the protection with strong metal links called Carabiners (sometimes called Carabineers), often described as "a small yet strong device, the mighty carabiners serve many crucial roles in safe climbing." [15]

I believe we can find a spiritual correlation in Ephesians chapter 6, where Paul writes that above all we are supposed to take "the shield of faith with which you will be able to quench all the fiery darts of the wicked one." (Ephesians 6:16) I am convinced faith acts as our strong carabiner.

Faith is the bridge that connects us to our invisible expectations. Our faith is linked to our trust in Christ. He is the one that has gone before us. Faith is not just an assumption that the lead climber knows what he is doing. The carabiners are anchored in the reality of Christ's (our lead climber) capability (power), His provision (what He has made available) and His promise (what He promised to do). They are directly linked to the truth of the Word of God (the rope) and Christ is the Word of God. (John 1:1-3) Stewart Green and Ian Spencer-Green write that "The function and use of this technical climbing gear is purely based on the lead climber's knowledge of how to use it [carabineers]." [16]

The writer of the book of Hebrews connects this perfectly for us, "Seeing then that we have a great high priest, that is passed into the heavens, Jesus the Son of God, let us hold fast our profession. For we have not an high priest which cannot be touched with the feeling of our infirmities; but was in all points tempted like as we are, yet without sin. Let us therefore come boldly unto the throne of grace that we may obtain mercy, and find grace to help in time of need." (Hebrews 4:14-16)(KJV) Boldness here means coming before God clothed in the righteousness of Christ. We are bold because Jesus Christ is the lead climber.

No wonder Christ urged us to have faith in God (some translations says faith of God). We are not moved by the size of the mountain before us because our faith is linked to Christ, the lead climber. Hebrews 11:1 says, "Now faith is the substance of things hoped for and the evidence of things not seen." (KJV) Using a mountain climber's perspective, I believe it means that faith is the substance of my expectations in Christ anchored by the unfailing evidence of His unseen presence in my climb to the summit. Romans 1:17 says "the just shall live by faith." (KJV) I don't see any other way to live. I have not found a better definition of faith than the one offered by Pastor James Ford, "Faith is your soul seeing what your eyes cannot, your heart believing what your mind will not and your will accepting what your common sense says you should not." [17]

Finally, the last essential kit necessary for mountain climbing we will examine is what Brandon Mathis calls the emergency kit. He writes, "An essential mountain climber's arsenal is the emergency kit. Typical emergency/first aid items like matches, small bandages and ointments are a necessity. … Many emergency kits come with a small plastic mirror to reflect light and catch attention." [18] Here again we turn to Paul for a correlative spiritual kit, "praying always with all prayer and supplication in the Spirit, being watchful to this end with all perseverance and supplication for all the saints." (Ephesians 6:18)

A mountain climber's emergency kit reflects the light to guide other climbers. Paul said we should pray and make supplication for all saints and not for ourselves. Many prayers I hear this day are for "me, myself and I". Mountain climbing is strangely a team sport. In the vertical journey to the summit, the sojourners at the top and those coming behind are all interlinked by the same rope. (Christ, the Word) We have to pray for one another and encourage one another.

The emergency kit only contains the essentials, as you cannot afford to carry too much baggage. Mountain climbers travel light. You cannot afford to have hindrances such as unforgiveness and bitterness against fellow climbers or anyone at all. The Psalmist says if I regard iniquity in my heart, the Lord will not hear me. (Psalm 66:18) Supplication means to make a humble entreaty to God and request divine intervention in the journey to the summit.

With all your gear in place, it is time to start the journey and begin climbing with purpose, conviction and determination, bracing against all odds and any kind of weather, knowing Christ is our lead climber. But how do we walk? We have to "walk circumspectly, not as fools but as wise, redeeming the time, because the days are evil. Wherefore be ye not unwise, but understanding what the will of the Lord is." (Ephesians 5:15-17)(KJV)

We are to walk light. Mathis writes that the experienced modern climber's baggage is very light. "Many climbers prefer an internal-frame pack. These bags have frames that are inside the construction of the pack, often made from lightweight plastics. They are narrow and tall instead of short and wide, keeping weight close to your body, allowing for more natural and unencumbered movements while climbing ... expedition mountaineers will diligently pack equipment based on importance, accessibility and weight." [19]

We are to cast away all things that are unfruitful works and "do not be entangled again with a yoke of bondage." (Galatians 5:1) Don't struggle with baggage that only weighs you down and hinders your progress to the mountaintop. Get help in reducing the baggage if you have attachment issues with its contents. Get rid of stuff that is not necessary, even some necessities that are not essentials need to be cast away. Trust God to take you through, He is always the Great Provider. What are necessities in the valley may count for nothing as you journey up the mountain. The older we get, the less appealing the stuff we cling to in our juvenile years appears.

In this chapter, we learned about the need to be forearmed in facing the battles of life. But the gear we need should fit with the task ahead and the environment. The gear must fit the terrain, the inclement weather and most importantly, the challenge before us. Spiritually, we find that the Bible encourages us to put on the whole armor of God in fighting the battles of life. Now that we have the proper gear, it is time to set out for the summit, so let's get the team ready. Christ has already shown us the way.

PRINCIPLES

1. You need more than just the will to climb a mountain to reach the summit.

2. The same principle applies to both figurative and physical mountains: Without the necessary tools, hardware and gear, one can easily be blown away by inclement weather and difficult mountain terrains.

3. A person who carries emotional baggage through life is not going to go far on the journey to the mountaintop.

4. The baggage of hurt, bitterness, jealousy and pain cuts across cultures, peoples and individuals even though not all of us carry the same amount of baggage.

5. What do you have to tender to God?

6. Put on the whole armor of God that you may be able to stand against the wiles of the devil.

7. The Word of the Lord you receive is what will keep you going in the day of need.

8. The protection afforded by the harness (Word of God) helps keep you from drifting away or getting lost on the cliffs as you climb.

9. Call it the Word, a rope, or a belt or a sword, all I ask is never leave home without it.

10. Spiritually, I am convinced the helmet of salvation is a strong metaphor for the protection of the soul through the light of the gospel of Christ.

11. Shod your feet with the gospel of peace, peace with God, peace with men and peace with ourselves.

12. Faith acts as our strong carabiner. Faith is the bridge that connects us to our invisible expectations.

13. A mountain climber's emergency kit reflects the light to guide other climbers. Paul said we should pray and make supplication for all saints and not just for ourselves only.

14. Travel light, take only the essentials.

DISCUSSION GUIDE

1. What is in your backpack?

2. Discuss what emotional baggage and physical baggage mean in this chapter in the light of the Word of God.

3. How can you protect yourself, your family and your church from falling debris from the mountains, spiritual wickedness and the rulers of darkness?

4. List all of the pieces of God's armor as stated by the Apostle Paul and find any correlation between them and our modern sports or military gear. Why are they necessary?

CHAPTER SEVEN
MOUNTAINEERING IS A TEAM SPORT –
CHOOSE YOUR TEAM WISELY

*Erik says he doesn't want to be the Blind Climber. He wants to be a good
climber, a full team member who pulls his weight on a big mountain. "I am
living proof of the promise of teamwork, and the need for teamwork."*
– Mark Obmascik [1]

When Erik Weihenmayer, the first blind climber to scale Mount Everest and the
highest peak on each of the seven continents was asked by Mark Obsmascik why
he still climbed, even after the seven summits, he said among other things that he
loves the camaraderie, the bonding, "the work, tears, feeling of accomplishment,
the feel of the wind and the sound of the rocks, the taste of his sweat when he
thinks he can't go any farther but still does. Most of all, he loves when people
tell him he can't do something, and then he does it anyway." [2] What he apparently
forgot to mention is the unresolved question on how the mountain came to be
and why our passion to succeed exists in us in the first place. I respectfully submit
that God puts that desire in each one of us. He is the one that allows the mountain
to stay in place, but that is not exactly the focus of this section.

Erik went blind at thirteen years of age and took up rock climbing in a gym
because he could feel his way up the walls. He had a friend who found that
climbing helped his Attention Deficit Disorder (ADD), so they started climbing
together, the guy who couldn't see physically and the guy who couldn't focus
mentally.

When he announced his plans to climb Mount Everest, the entire
mountaineering world recoiled in horror, not at the thought of a blind man
on the world's tallest peak but the danger and risk he posed to himself and
his team members. He defied all the naysayers, and pursued his dream. He
summited Mount Everest on May 25, 2001, making the cover of Time, Outside
and Climbing magazines. His autobiography sold more than 350,000 copies.
Erik's hiking partner leads the way in all their climbs by dangling a bell from his
backpack. Erik simply follows the jingle. Obsmascik reports that he remains a
pretty normal person with an unusually small ego despite his world record setting
mountaineering achievements, all of which he attributes to teamwork. [3]

There are many mountains that you cannot climb by yourself. The world
revolves around relationships including your relationship with Christ and your
relationship with others. You cannot overcome your mountainous problems
until you get your relationships right. As we stated earlier, sometimes the process

and procedures of mountain climbing are more important than the substantive mountaintop experience.

You need wisdom in choosing your teammate for the task ahead. While it is true that you need help to get over some mountains in your life, what you need is more than a warm body. You need to surround yourself with spiritually attuned people, people that are well grounded in spiritual mountaineering. They need to be tried and tested companions and teammates with the peculiar knowledge of the tortuous route that leads to the mountaintop. There is no other team leader than Christ, the Son of God. Most people fail at life because of lack of support or the inability to honor commitment. People often surround themselves with folks who will take them further away from the summit of their mountain or those who will get them bogged down in a local relief.

As Cloud and Thompson once said, "These non-helpful people are not necessarily bad people …the reality is that some friends and acquaintances are not able to do the things that our community is supposed to do for us." [4] They may be fun to have around, they make your life hilariously funny when they are around you but they will never get you to where you want to go. Some of them may like you but they add nothing to you.

Climbers often travel in community. They know each other and travel like a band of brothers and sisters. You have to pick your mountain companions wisely as your community of friends in the valley may turn out to be a drag when you try to negotiate the difficult path to the summit of your mountainous challenge. The fact that they are close to you in the valley does not necessarily qualify them for the arduous task of mountain climbing. You have to weed out those who do not belong in your community through wisdom and divine direction. Those who are ill suited for climbing will be a drag on your upward climb. Even more dangerous are those who will not just bog you down but may actually drag you backward with them.

Life is relational by design. The Lord God said, "It is not good that man should be alone; I will make him a helper comparable to him." (Genesis 2:18) We need to learn to pick the best people, or to use the language of the Himalayas, "Sherpas" for our community.

There is a moving story of a paralytic man in the Bible. He could not walk or move; he was severely limited in mobility. This is one of the first miracles in the New Testament. The Bible says Jesus was surrounded by a large crowd of people, so this man stood no chance of being noticed by the miracle worker, Jesus. But four of his friends carried him to the roof of the house where Jesus was healing the sick. They first removed the roof and then lowered him down in front of Jesus. The Bible says, seeing their faith, Jesus said to the paralytic man, "pick up your pallet and go home" and he got up immediately. This was an extraordinary miracle of breakthrough for this man and his friends played a huge role in helping him overcome his inadequacies. Many people are stuck at the foot of their mountains because they are too ashamed to ask for help; while some are trying to climb rocks and mountains they are ill-equipped to climb nor endowed to surmount.

We need to understand that there are some mountains you are meant to climb and there are others you have to speak to and command to move. If you try to climb the mountains you are meant to speak to and command to move, you may die trying to climb its many local reliefs for your labor is in vain. If you try to speak to, command and move a mountain you are empowered to climb, you will cry yourself hoarse trying to speak to a mountain planted by God in your path to mold you and make your journey more fulfilling. Many live their lives in frustration and guilt, feeling sorry for themselves at the foot of their mountain not knowing what to do.

There are other mountains you need a combination of the two strategies to overcome. For instance, sin and guilt. No matter how much you try, you can't get rid of the feelings of guilt and despondency you feel when you commit a sin except through genuine repentance and forgiveness which comes through the blood of Jesus. Jesus Christ said, "Come to me, all you who labor and are heavy laden, and I will give you rest." (Matthew 11:28) Still many people are perpetually feeling sorry for themselves rather than laying it down at the feet of Jesus.

John, one of the disciples of Jesus, put it succinctly, "If we confess our sins, He is faithful and just to forgive us our sins and to cleanse us from all unrighteousness." (I John 1:9) In Proverbs 28:13, the Bible says, "He who conceals his transgressions will not prosper. But he who confesses and forsakes them will find compassion." (NASB) In other words, calling and relying on Jesus' blood for the propitiation of our sins is as important as His command for us to confess our sins. We have to accept Christ's help and confess our sins to have mercy. It is time we stop trying to climb a mountain not meant for us to ascend alone. No matter the nature of your sin and guilt, the good news I have for you is that the blood of Jesus cleanses from all sins. (I John 1:7) In choosing your community of climbers, Jesus should be your number one team member.

Every successful person in the world today rose on the shoulders of those who have gone before them. No man is an island to himself. God will always direct you to gifted people or direct gifted people to you. You must learn to recognize them when you meet them.

One of the world's foremost soccer coaches is Jose Mourinho. He is among the rare cerebral coaches who have won the top national soccer league cup in three European countries and has also won the European Champions League Cup twice. Many people are surprised that this genius of a soccer coach never played the game professionally. When asked about the secret of his success, he often attributes his knowledge of the game to his apprenticeship under the legendary English soccer coach, Sir Bobby Robson. Today Mourinho has achieved more than Robson's greatest dreams.

You need to be around the right people, and not necessarily supermen or women. Tiger Woods sought help in changing his swing from those who had never won a single PGA tour. (Not once, but twice!) And he became better on each occasion. Conversely, the team of advisers, sycophants and leeches he surrounds himself with contributed to his downfall and the failure of his marriage. It was reported that none of his advisers counseled him on his out of control behavior. They were too beholden to him to question his judgment and decisions. They simply looked the other way while he destroyed his home. You need people around you who will tell you the truth!

Your climbing community partners may just show up in your life when you least expect it or you may have to align yourself with them. No matter how and where they appear in your life, it will be self-evident that God brought all of you together. Remember though that there is no "I" in team, and "m" (call it "me" if you like) is the last letter in TEAM! The mistake we often make is that we look for those who look like us, who speak like us and think like us and then make them our community partners when God is asking us to climb with a diverse group of people some of whom will inevitably rub us the wrong way to make us better.

To find good partners, be one yourself.

In climbing your mountainous challenge, be prepared to team up with people I once called "sandpaper" people. They are people who will rub you the wrong way, speak the truth to your face and generally make you ill at ease when you sin. They may not necessarily come from your church or workplace. What they bring to you is the gift, the anointing and influence you need to get to the top of your mountain.

You should never mistake the bearer of gifts with the gift giver. God is the giver of all gifts. No matter how influential someone may be in your life, never make them your God. Your team members bring to the table a multitude of gifts and you need the safety net that love, support and affection bring to your life. A strong partnership and a good community gives us feedback based on their experience and reminds us of the importance of our core values while holding us accountable for our actions as we journey through the mountains of life. Our core values must be grounded in God's infallible word found in the Bible.

Nathan taught David accountability through a riddle. Jethro taught Moses delegated authority and public administration. Titus encouraged Paul and provided companionship as he journeyed through the mountains of persecution. "Two are better than one, because they have a good reward for their labor. For if they fall, one will lift up his companion. But woe to him who is alone when he falls. For he has no one to help him up." (Ecclesiastes 4:9-10)

I was listening to a podcast interview with one of the greatest rock climbers in the world, Alex Honnold. He spoke with sadness about the loss of a fellow rock climber, legendary free solo adventurer, John Bachar. A man that had climbed and successfully climbed many steep rocks fell to his death at a rock near his home in Mammoth Lakes, California. [5]

Ecclesiastes 4:11-12 continues, "Again if two lie down together, they will keep warm; But how can one be warm alone? Though one may be overpowered by another, two can withstand him; And a threefold cord is not quickly broken." There are people who are stagnant in their outlook on life, and there are others who are growing and developing. You need as traveling companions people with the desire and drive to grow and go beyond their current level. Stagnant people will never advance your dream; they will bring you down to their level. Aspiring people are constantly looking for a way to make themselves and others around them better.

My first son, Sammy, was at a critical point in his life when he entered high school as a freshman. He plodded through middle school struggling with all kinds of adolescent issues. He looked for relevance and companionship from friends who dragged him down to their level. As a result, his grades suffered and plunged to levels that he himself could not imagine.

When he got to high school, Sammy met a group of seniors on the cross country athletic team that were willing to take him under their wing and mentor him. Immediately his grades improved and he became so disciplined that he was waking up early to go on runs, coming back from school to sit down, read and prepare for his homework and tests. I could not believe his transformation.

Some people fail at life because of lack of support or the inability to honor commitment. [6] Some surround themselves with people who will invariably take them further away from their mountain's summit or cause them to get bogged down on the way up. Cloud and Townsend said, "There are two traveling companions' dangers: the absence of good supporters and the presence of those who hurt our cause." [7] We need to know how to pick the best people for our community, because very often it is only the people with the best team that wins. There are many people who are scared of taking risks. Those who play not to lose often fail spectacularly.

Friendship and relationship make all the difference on a team. You can afford to go a small distance with people you don't have much of a relationship with but you can't take that risk with long-term climbing partners. I asked my friend, the rock climber, about mentorship in climbing. He said the reason why mentorship often fails in climbing sports is that many mentees want to get to the summit before they learn the ropes. He said "many of them want to skip steps and just get to the summit, instead of starting at the basics and then move up." [8]

Trust is an important requirement for partners in mountaineering and rock climbing, because you are implicitly putting your entire life in the hands of your partner. Someone once described faith as a five year old flying down from a bunk bed as soon as he sees his dad, trusting that his dad will catch him before he hits the ground.

All climbers, except solo venturers, need someone to catch them. You pick such people carefully. My friend said among experienced climbers who travel out of their localities to climb, all it takes to find a trusted partner is 5-10 minutes of conversation. "Most of the folks that end up at the top of summit know each other from those who just talk about climbing, but never really do it. The higher you get to the top of the rock, or mountain, the easier it is to trust people that are on their way up." [9]

My rock climbing friend said the most contentious partnership he has seen on the road is a husband and wife team. They fight often and rarely agree because of their individual competitive spirits. Success at home will definitely impact your climbing goals. A good home life is crucial to stress-free climbing. It is often difficult for a husband and wife to give each other honest feedback. You need your spouse to be less of a cheerleader and more of an evaluator.

There is also a distinct difference between bragging about your success and inspiring others with your achievements, pride versus humility. A proud man imagines himself as doing or being anything, he even believes he can fly, but the law of gravity will surely nip his pride in the bud. However, with humility, you take a broader view of how your actions will affect others.

I asked my friend, what are the markers we need to keep in mind when picking a good partner? He started out by saying, avoid talkers. In the climbing community, they are often called "sprayers" because they spray you with what they can do but not so much what they have done. They are often not ready to pay the price that it will take to get to the summit. They are also called "posers" in the climbing community (we call them "Alan Poser" in Nigeria). You will find them in the valley talking about the many difficult routes they have traveled to the tallest mountains and rocks in the world and yet their backpacks look fresh and new. They will regal you with what you cannot do but rarely make any attempt to leave the foothills themselves. As you leave base camp, they will be chatting up a new set of people as they remain in the foothills. If you can picture yourself at the top of the mountain, then you must be ready to visualize every move that will get you there.

The next people to avoid are those who do a victory lap midway to the top forgetting that the destination is still far away. Yes, by all means celebrate small achievements, however, don't overdo it. We will come back to this issue in subsequent chapters. For now, suffice it to say, lazy people should also be avoided at all costs along with arrogant people. I think the reason for their exclusion on your team is self explanatory.

So how can we pick the right people? Who should be part of our circle of climbers? Of course, the first partner should be Jesus, the author and finisher of our faith. When you make Jesus the captain of the team, He will set the standards and the rules of engagement. For instance He said in Matthew 6:25-34 that we should seek the Kingdom and its righteousness and then every other thing would be added unto us.

Partnership starts with self-examination, whatever you demand of others you must be ready and willing to inculcate in yourself. Expand your field and tastes. Sometimes what we think is important may not necessarily be that important. Be open to climbing with people you would not normally have on your list. Don't try to impress others with pretensions. Be yourself. Long lasting intimacy is impossible where there is pretense. Don't unnecessarily suspect and ascribe motives to others.

More importantly, to find good partners, be one yourself. Be faithful to the assignment, be devoted to the task, be honest and sincere with yourself and others, and let them find you to be trustworthy and dependable. In Luke 16:10-12, Jesus Christ said faithfulness starts with little things, then money, and finally, how we handle other people's property. Yes, God provides for the little sparrows, but sometimes, the little bird still has to leave her nest to find the divinely provided food. He that wants a friend must show himself friendly. (Proverbs 18:24a)

Network with friends, family and your community. Join others with the same interests. You must sow seeds of friendship to harvest friends. Love passionately but set boundaries and let people know the task is more important than the fun. Be patient with others. Tolerate the pain of learning without enabling an attitude of failure. Above all, stay connected with the herd. Remember the sheep that wanders away is the one that gets eaten by the wolves.

Every relationship will suffer the inevitable bump. We need to learn to resolve our differences without being unnecessarily disagreeable. (Romans 12:18) To resolve your differences, begin with God. Speak the truth to each other in love. Admit when you are wrong. Find people you respect to mediate. Be honest with your position. Don't pursue a position that seeks nothing but the humiliation of your partner. Proverbs 19:11 says "The discretion of a man makes him slow to anger, and his glory is to overlook a transgression." When you win an argument, reach out a hand of fellowship and when you lose, admit it and move on. Remember, relationships can either build you up or pull you down. Love deeply and carefully. Above all, avoid toxic people, they will poison your spirit and kill your dreams. But imperfect people are not necessarily toxic people. [10] If you look in the mirror, you will see your own imperfections. Seek good people who will celebrate you as well as tell you when you get it wrong.

I met my wife for the first time at Nigeria's National Youth Service Corps Orientation Boot Camp at St. Patrick's College, Asaba, Nigeria. I was actually drawn to her through her friend who was the object of my friend's desire and affection. I was trying to help my friend get the attention of her friend when I noticed her. At the end of the boot camp, we both exchanged addresses like all other Christian Youth Corpers. We kept in touch through the Corpers' Fellowship. As she was based in Umunede and I was in Asaba, she often had to travel to Asaba, the state capital for official and fellowship functions. On such occasions, we hosted her and other brothers from out of town at our living quarters.

During Christmas break, I sent greetings cards to everyone and she was the only one that responded. Towards the end of the service year, I approached her pastor about my affection and desire for her. He gave me the go-ahead to talk to her. I traveled to her location and proposed to her. I have always been someone that eschews long courtships, not because I had anything against them, but because I seriously doubted my own emotional ability to withhold physical affection for long. I told her about my plan to marry her within two years of settling down in Lagos, Nigeria.

At the Corps' final parade, the state made a serious error on my discharge certificate and it was such that it would have delayed my opportunity to secure a job and affect my future. I met her as I was being handed my certificate. She looked at it and immediately ran to the Corps officials and requested to see the calligrapher. They said none was available and that they had to send the certificate to Abuja (Nigeria's national capital, thousands of miles from Asaba) for correction. She asked me to follow her, as she proceeded to speak directly and confidently with the State Director of the program.

> *To maximize team performance, we will need to create the appropriate culture, values, ethos, and a process that is clear and uncluttered along with a commitment sealed by loyalty and a determination strengthened by purpose.*

To this day, I don't know where they found a calligrapher but they did make the required changes to my discharge certificate. That yeoman's effort on her part remained indelible in my memory. Later in our marriage, I drew upon this event along with other memories when my wife did something that hurt my feelings.

I am grateful I married someone that cares deeply about me and our children. She is constantly thinking of how to shore up our finances, prepare for the children's education and provide for our home. Long before I met her, I had asked God to give me someone that perfectly complemented me. My passion is to see my children succeed and to be there for my children, maybe because my parents were not really "there" for me.

I was determined to suffer any hardship, endure any pain, deny any comfort as long as my children had the opportunities that I never had. I also asked God to give me someone that knew and understood mathematics and science. Because of my liberal arts background, I knew my limitations in those areas. The thought of my children asking for help with mathematics and science homework, which I cannot answer or understand, frightened me. It was therefore a thing of joy when she told me she graduated with a degree in microbiology. There were other attributes I wanted my wife to have which she sorely lacked when we first got married, but as time went on, I discovered that once she realized the importance of those areas to me, she began improving on them.

I also had to adjust to meet her specific desires. One thing she wanted in her husband was someone that cares for and loves her children. She said God answered her prayer. Because her father was tall, my wife asked God to give her a husband that was tall and gangly. Unfortunately, I was not too tall and not too short. She struggled with this but later accepted it, when she discovered other qualities she now admires in me which weren't on her list. These qualities are actually now more important to her than the physical features she had been asking God to provide in her husband.

I also found that because my wife lost her father at a very early age, she was overly concerned about every detail of my health. In fact, sometimes it bordered on being "overly anxious". When I discovered this, I made sure that I did my utmost to allay her fears about my health and assure her prayerfully that our life is in God's hands and He had promised that with long life will He satisfy us. (Psalm 91:16)

There is no doubt that my wife is a good team member as we undertake our journey through the mountains of life. We support each other, comfort each other and look out for one another. When we are separated by long distance due to education or other reasons, we have implicit confidence that nothing will impinge on our love for each other.

Complementing our strength with the strength of others greatly increased our chance of success. As Coach Tony Dungy once stated, "The kind of people we had on our team would affect our ability to get the result we wanted." [11]

In addition to friend and confidante, we also need within our team: 1. a dream validator: Jesus did not start His ministry by proclaiming Himself as the Son of God. John the Baptist saw and testified that He was the Son of God. (John 1:34) 2. a burden sharer: an Elizabeth that will come alongside of you to strengthen you in the time of need, encourage you when people make fun of you, and, 3. a witness, that will help pass on your legacy and confirm your dream. (I Samuel 1:11-18) All the characteristics of a good team member we have examined will count for nothing if those who surround us lack good character.

Character is the glue that binds and solidifies all successful relationships. Get connected to a community of healthy, stable, loving, honest climbers. Make them your family, where you struggle together, care for one another, mourn together, endure together, and celebrate together. We can always achieve more with a team than without. [12]

To maximize team performance, we will need to create the appropriate culture, values, ethos, and a process that is clear and uncluttered along with a commitment sealed by loyalty and a determination strengthened by purpose. Most often, efficient, high-performing teams have a high level of diversity, sustainability and nurturing culture. The culture you create around your team will permeate every member and every relationship.

Above all, remember, Christ in us is the hope of glory. Jesus is the model for every relationship. He set boundaries for multitudes, disciples and His inner circle. He sets the standard for His friends. He points all His friends and acquaintances towards His Heavenly Father. He is friend to the rich, the poor, the publican and rulers of the synagogue. He visited and dined with tax collectors. He appointed all kinds of people to His cabinet/team. He loves children, the elderly, the infirmed, the blind and disabled. He is not shy to rebuke those who abuse the House of God and yet hears the cries of demons for a proper place for relocation. He receives guests in the dead of night and He talks with prostitutes. He judged people based on their actions and not preconceived notions. He even allows His betrayer to eat from the same plate with Him.

He leads His team by example and not by force. He will help you get your team together. He is the only one that can complete us. He is the way to the summit of your mountain. He is the truth you are seeking to fulfill. He is the life that will sustain you in your time of need. The grace of God is more than sufficient. There is nothing more to add at this point than to wish you "au revoir". Farewell. Remember Paul's prayer to the Corinthians, "Be of good comfort, be of one mind, live in peace; and the God of love and peace will be with you." (II Corinthians 13:11)

PRINCIPLES

1. There are many mountains that you cannot climb alone.

2. Life is relational by design. (Genesis 2:18)

3. The world revolves around relationships, your relationship with Christ and your relationship with others.

4. You need wisdom in choosing your teammates for the task ahead.

5. Climbers often travel in community.

6. Extricate yourself from those who do not belong in your community through wisdom and divine direction.

7. Many people are stuck at the foot of their mountains because they are too ashamed to ask for help. And others are attempting to climb rocks and mountains they are ill-equipped to climb nor endowed to surmount.

8. Accept Christ's help and confess your sins to receive mercy. It is time we stop trying to climb a mountain not meant for us to ascend alone.

9. Every successful person in the world today built and rose on the shoulders of those who have gone before them.

10. Your climbing community partners may just show up in your life when you least expect them or you may have to align yourself with them.

11. Sandpaper people will rub you the wrong way, speak the truth to your face and generally make you ill at ease when you sin.

12. No matter how influential someone may be in your life, never make them your God.

13. A strong partnership and a good community give us feedback based on their experience and remind us of the importance of our core values while holding us accountable for our actions as we journey through the mountains of life.

14. Some people fail at life because of lack of support or the inability to honor commitment.

15. Trust is an important requirement for partners in mountaineering and rock climbing.

16. There is a distinct difference between bragging about your success and inspiring others with your achievements.

17. Partnership starts with self-examination, whatever you demand of others you must be ready and willing to inculcate in yourself.

18. To find good partners, be one yourself. Be faithful to the assignment, be devoted to the task, be honest and sincere with yourself and others, and let them find you to be trustworthy and dependable.

19. Network with friends, family and your community. Join others with the same interests. You must sow seeds of friendship to harvest friends.

20. Every relationship will suffer the inevitable bump. We need to learn to resolve our differences without being unnecessarily disagreeable.

21. Complementing our strength with the strength of others greatly increases our chance of success.

22. Character is the glue that binds and solidifies all successful relationships.

23. To maximize team performance, we will need to create the appropriate culture, values, ethos, and a process that is clear and uncluttered along with a commitment sealed by loyalty and a determination strengthened by purpose.

24. Above all, remember Christ in us is the hope of glory. Jesus is the model for every relationship.

DISCUSSION GUIDE

1. How can we pick the right people?

2. Who should be part of our circle of climbers?

3. How did Jesus pick his team?

4. How can we set the standard of God with our friends without being a jerk?

5. Are we always required to please people so as not to appear disagreeable?

Part III
Mountain Climbing

Stop complaining about what you don't have or what you need for a perfect journey, use what you have to get to your goal.

CHAPTER EIGHT
BEGIN YOUR JOURNEY NOW

It takes a certain amount of time to prepare for a game and once we're prepared, extra time won't help – only execution will.
–Tony Dungy, retired NFL coach [1]

The time we spend in preparation and team formation is crucial in a mountain climb and is particularly necessary in surmounting all the problematic mountains in our lives. While it is important to pack the right stuff in our backpack and assemble the right team, we must never get so caught up with the planning process that preparation becomes an end in itself. We must know when to start marching up the mountain. At the "burning bush", God revealed to Moses only his general plan and intent to deliver the children of Israel from Egypt. The details about the Red Sea crossing, water in the desert and manna to combat their hunger et al. were not given to him.

Once we hear the "go" of Christ, any other excuses about waiting on God for details is just what they are, EXCUSES! Our best plans won't survive the first grind against an obstacle or the enemy. Not everything that we face on the journey to the top can be successfully predicted, there isn't a game plan for every situation. No obstacle can be overcome until it is faced. Go! Do! Act! Ascend!

It was about two years after my family and I had settled into our new home in Spokane, Washington and life was pretty good. My temporary/seasonal job was now permanent with the City of Spokane. My wife had joined me, together with our three little children, about 11 months earlier. Things were not as bad as when we were living in Washington DC. We tried to settle down in Spokane as best we could. Our children were enrolled in a very good public elementary school. We loved our neighbors and church family. After several unsuccessful attempts to secure a laboratory scientist job at a local biochemistry firm, my wife began working as a nursing assistant at a senior center near our home. Everything was "dandy dandy" as we used to call it in Nigeria but then one night my wife woke me up in the middle of the night and said she would like to tell me something important.

I asked, "Can't it wait till tomorrow?" in between sleep deprived yawns and heavy eyes.

"No, it can't wait," she said.

I immediately sat up. All kinds of thoughts were racing through my head as I wondered what I said to her during the day that might have rubbed her the wrong way. She sensed my worries and immediately began to reassure me that we had no crisis or emergency.

"I would like to go back to school and do my Licensed Professional Nursing program in Washington DC," she stated, with a deadpan look on her face, as she studied me intently.

I immediately realized that this was not a statement thrown out for deliberation but had been carefully thought out with determined resolve. If there is one thing I know about my wife, she rarely wakes up in the middle of the night. She loves to sleep and if she were to wake up for a conversation then I needed to wake up, too. My wife would brook no sleepy hubby when an important matter dear to her needed to be aired. On the other hand, I was at a loss for words to respond to her request.

"Can we have this discussion tomorrow?" I asked.

She said, "I have put a great deal of thought into this and I'm ready to go."

I tried to convince her to continue with her ongoing program at Spokane Community College.

"I don't stand a chance of making the waiting list for the nursing program."

I said, "Good. I am willing to support you for as long as it takes." I wrapped my arms around her and we went back to sleep.

Days went by, followed by weeks and months and I never heard anything more about it. At one point, I just gave up on her talking about it again. About three months later, we were having a conversation about one of my son's penchant for postponing his assignments until the eleventh hour and I said something to the effect that I was glad he didn't get that from me. My wife looked at me with a penetrating eye and then walked away.

"Nobody made a greater mistake than he who did nothing because he could only do a little." – Edmund Burke

The following day, unbeknownst to me, she called our family friend in Washington DC and bought a plane ticket. She started the Licensed Professional Nursing program that month. Even though I tried to deal with the situation as best I could by withholding money from her, my wife procured a credit card and used it to enroll in classes.

She left me with three kids but assured me that all would be well. My wife promised to come home frequently. It still amazes our family friend that hosted her in DC, how she was able to do it. My friend's wife was so touched by her determination that soon after my wife's graduation she closed down her small party picnic hosting and cooking business and completed the same nursing program.

After completing the LPN program, my wife got a job working for a nursing home in Spokane. This job immediately increased our income and we were a lot more comfortable. We were able to support our siblings in Nigeria with school fees and send a small allowance to other family members in Nigeria.

Then one day, my wife started talking about enrolling in the Registered Nursing program at a community college in Spokane. I immediately thought about the impact the reduced income would have on our finances and tried to dissuade her. I told her that her company may not take kindly to her going back to school and taking time away from work when they were so short-staffed.

"I'll look into it," she said.

Three days later, she told me that her employer had approved her request to change her shift to the afternoon so she could go to school. I raised another potential obstacle with regards to where we would keep the kids after school as we did not qualify for the paid school Express Program. My wife agreed to work extra hours on the weekend to pay for it.

Lo, and behold, she started the program and completed the program in record time without delay. Again our finances increased and it helped us greatly. The seemingly impossible task becomes possible when you stop procrastinating and take the first step. We all have to learn to distinguish between "can't" and "won't", between "will" and "do". Those who adapt to the seasons, rather than demand that the seasons adapt to them will reap in due time. [2]

We have all heard the saying that the journey of a thousand miles starts with one step. It is very true, particularly with mountain climbing. I had planned to write this book for several years. I kept pushing it back. The interesting thing is that every time I thought about it, I almost always had a "good" excuse to put it off. Finally in January 2013, I listened to an online podcast by Bishop Tudor Bismark titled, "Establishing Dominion". [3] In the message, he was talking about how God fulfilled his promise to Abraham, but then he suddenly went off topic and started talking about carrying out our assignment. He said something to the effect, "Go do it. Go write that book! Stop dilly dallying around!", at least that is what I heard. At the end of that day, I picked up my wife's laptop and wrote the first 3 chapters of this book.

As Blaise Pascal, once intoned, "The least movement is of importance to all nature. The entire ocean is affected by a pebble." [4] Stop complaining about what you don't have or what you need for a perfect journey to attain your dream. Do something about the mountain of problems in front of you, act and make the situation better. I think it was Edmund Burke that was quoted as saying that "nobody made a greater mistake than he who did nothing because he could only do a little." [5]

When God directs our path to our mountain, He very often may not give us the timeline it will take to get to the summit. This is because most divine assignments are not a time critical competition on the blast of a gun. Life is not necessarily like an Olympic 100 meter sprint race. God is more interested in our growth on the journey to the mountain than how quickly we make it up there. Even though God works in our lives within time and expects us to redeem the time, He is not going to judge us based on timing. Yes, He is an eternal God that is not bound by time, but He will always fulfill His promises to you within time.

Much of life is moving from mountain to mountain, the earlier you embrace your assignment the better. Look upward, draw deeply inward and propel yourself to greater heights as you take on the challenges of life.

Never detest the day of small beginnings. Recognize and appreciate your small beginnings. Successful and long lasting marital relationships start with couples who celebrate each other's small beginnings. While moving on higher and higher, keep your eyes on little details and small things that may trip you up later. David never forgot the sheep even after he was anointed king by Samuel. (I Samuel 17:20) God is not going to judge you on killing Goliath but your care for the few sheep. We should never despise or disrespect the foothills where we learn the ropes. Always be enthusiastic about the assignment. Like David, we should find joy in the few sheep put in our care. (I Samuel 17:20, 28)

You have started your journey to the summit, but remember it is an endurance test, and not a sprint. Always celebrate little achievements on the way. Appreciate the small moments as much as the big wins. Keep going. There will be damage, there will be injuries, there will be pain but remember God is a God of fresh starts and renewal. He will renew your strength. Isaiah 40:31 says, "But those who wait on the Lord shall renew their strength; they shall mount up with wings like eagles, they shall run and not be weary, they shall walk and not faint."

PRINCIPLES

1. Do not get so caught up in the planning process that preparation becomes an end in itself.

2. Your best survival plans may not survive the first grind against an obstacle or the enemy, be it hunger, lack, or an attack by wild animals.

3. No obstacle can be overcome until it is faced. Go! Do! Act! Ascend!

4. The seemingly impossible task becomes possible when you stop procrastinating and take the first step.

5. We all have to learn to distinguish between "can't" and "won't", between "will" and "do".

6. Those who adapt to the seasons rather than demand that the seasons adapt to them will reap in due time.

7. Stop complaining about what you don't have or what you need for a perfect journey to attain your dream.

8. Like blind Bartimaeus, use what you have (voice) to get what you don't have (eyes).

9. Most divine assignments are not a time-critical competition on the blast of a gun.

10. God is more interested in our growth on the journey to the mountain than how quickly we make it up there.

11. Look upward, draw deeply inward and propel yourself to greater heights as you take on the challenges of life.

12. Never detest the day of small beginnings. Recognize and appreciate your small beginnings.

13. Appreciate the small moments as much as the big wins.

14. There will be damage, there will be injuries, there will be pain but remember God is a God of fresh starts and renewal. He will renew your strength.

15. Keep going.

DISCUSSION GUIDE

1. Itemize the task/projects you are planning to work on and critically examine what is holding you back from beginning the task.

2. Challenge each other on accomplishing tasks this week and see how each person did in getting focused or getting started.

3. What excuses are holding you back from fulfilling your destiny?

4. Before you make the list of what you don't have, start a list on what you have.

Once you allow fear to paralyze you and take over your thought process, it directs you to expect the worst outcome as the only plausible result.

CHAPTER NINE
MIDWAY UP THE MOUNTAIN: WHERE FEAR RULES, FAITH ELEVATES AND ENDURANCE UPLIFTS

*I know I'm not supposed to do it, but for the first time I look
back down the mountain. And I am horrified.*
– Mark Obmascik [1]

Hurray! You have made it to the midpoint of your mountain climb. You are not at the summit yet but you can see the glory ahead. You are excited and exhilarated. The truth is you never expected to come this far. The thought of arriving at this relief cliff, halfway up, makes you giddy. Unfortunately, this is the moment where we separate the men from the boys. As you look up, you can see the summit, but then someone or something catches your attention and you look back and freeze! Fear takes over – the fear of falling, the fear of the cliff's edge.

To tell you the truth, fears are unavoidable, whether it be the fear of failure or the fear of heights. Until the reason for our fears is addressed, it will remain perpetually an elephant in the room, or better yet, an elephant on the mountain! Jesus Christ knows you will be afraid, hence he told you, "let not your heart be troubled, you believe in God, believe also in me." (John 14:1) He also told you that if He can protect the little sparrow that flies to great heights, He can watch over you. "Do not fear therefore; you are of more value than many sparrows." (Matthew 10:31)

As you make your journey up the mountains of adversity, lack, poverty, hardship, turmoil, addiction or whatever it may be, the foothills or valleys of the status quo begin to recede from view. At that moment, fond memories of the past start drifting in. You are excited about what you left behind and then you look back and fear creeps in; the fear that you could trip up and be dashed headlong to an untimely death. Fear that you could end up losing all that you have worked hard for and go back to the "same old same old" or the fear that you are not good enough to make it all the way to the top.

The interesting thing here is that you might have planned on looking back to enjoy the view but fear took over. Fear is our natural emotional reaction to danger and problems. It warns us of impending catastrophe, no matter how irrational it may be. Immediately, our blood pressure goes up, the adrenaline kicks in and we begin to sweat, go numb and are paralyzed. Your stomach churns, heart palpitates and muscles tightened up. This is followed by mental and emotional paralysis. Irrational thoughts take over, as all you see are bad outcomes.

Recently I was watching a YouTube clip of Alex Honnold, one of the greatest solo rock climbers in the world, and widely acclaimed as the next great thing in modern climbing when something caught my attention. [2] He was on the edge of a rock at a midpoint, all of a sudden one of his cameramen recording the climb said something to him and he looked down to talk to him and he froze. This is one of the boldest and most courageous climbers in the world, yet he froze when he looked down from the midpoint. He had to stay at the spot for quite a while and gather himself, before he could resume the climb. Other folks plunge to their death at that point as fear paralyzes them.

Fear makes you forget all your preparation, testimony, and most importantly, your Source, God, who has called you to go and take on the giant. There is a reason why I Samuel 17 spends more time describing the 150 pounds of metal armor and weaponry on Goliath while a mere fleeting two verses is spent describing the entire army of Israel. That part of the passage was written from the viewpoint of an average recruit in Saul's army. All the Israelite soldiers saw looking across the Valley of Elah to the opposite mountain (I Samuel 17:2-3) was Goliath's bronze helmet, coat of mail, bronze armor, bronze javelin between his shoulders and iron spearheads. Fear turned them from warriors into spectators. (I Samuel 17: 5-7)

Their pitiable state is not helped by the lack of weapons in the arsenal of Israel's army. Let's see what they have. Other than Saul and Jonathan, none of the soldiers in Israel's army arrayed in battle against Goliath had a metal weapon as there were no blacksmiths throughout the land of Israel due to a deliberate policy of the Philistines. "So it came about, on the day of battle, that there was neither sword nor spear in the hand of any of the people who were with Saul and Jonathan." (I Samuel 13:19-22)

Ordinarily, anyone faced with such circumstances would panic and be very afraid, but thank God, David proved "the weapons of our warfare are not carnal, but mighty in God for pulling down strongholds." (II Corinthians 10:4) Sadly, Saul, Jonathan, Eliab and all the other men in battle, forgot that important fact. The Word of God you know is what will sustain you in the face of paralyzing fear.

Once you allow fear to paralyze you and take over your thought process, it directs you to expect the worst outcome as the only plausible result. Your debilitating fear convinces you to abandon your hopes and dreams. Panic attacks and anxiety take over which further hampers a good decision-making process. It is a classic "when it rains it pours" scenario. No wonder Jeremiah cautioned against anxiety, "For he shall be like a tree planted by the waters, Which spreads out its roots by the river, And will not fear when heat comes; But its leaf will be green, And will not be anxious in the year of drought, Nor will cease from yielding fruit." (Jeremiah 17:8) The key to victory over fear is to be planted by the waters; we know that water symbolizes the presence of the Holy Spirit.

Numbing and negative fear by itself is not the original purpose of fear in our life. God actually created and put fear in us as a positive mechanism to appreciate what we cannot control or mold, so He can shepherd us to safety and protect us from danger. That is why the fear of the Lord is the beginning of wisdom. Positive fear drives us away from danger and evil and draws us closer to God's kind love and affection which is a place of safety and security and saves our lives from perdition.

The negative force of fear is evil and deleterious to our health and sanity. It keeps us paralyzed and unable to act when God wants us to exercise our faith. When we panic and get anxious, our thinking process becomes completely paralyzed. This is probably the reason why the Bible says, "Be anxious for nothing, but in everything by prayer and supplication, with thanksgiving, let your requests be made known to God." (Philippians 4:6)

More importantly, we cease to take risks and act in faith when fear sets in. The very idea of self-preservation, which fear seeks to introduce in our lives, is antithetical to the very life Christ wants us to live. He said, "Whoever seeks to save his life will lose it, and whoever loses his life will preserve it." (Luke 17:33)

The key to understanding the better place to turn when fear comes is to first of all understand the important difference between healthy fears and harmful fears as examined through the lens of our everyday preparation and the Word of God. The truth is that both healthy fears and harmful fears come from our spirit. Our fears are influenced by the spiritual realm, either good or evil, and often affect the physical realm even though we cannot actually see them. Healthy fears, according to Isaiah 11:2, are often coupled with the Spirit of knowledge. "The Spirit of the Lord shall rest upon Him, the Spirit of wisdom and understanding, the Spirit of counsel and might, the Spirit of knowledge and

Our spirit and mind often operate like an inerasable video or DVD recorder with a huge memory disc which can easily burn fears into our subconscious.

of the fear of the Lord." (Isaiah 11:2) It is specifically geared towards making us delight in the "reverential" fear of the Lord (Isaiah 11:3) (AMP) and it is described as the root of wisdom. "The fear of the Lord is the beginning of wisdom, and the knowledge of the Holy One is understanding." (Proverbs 9:10) God in turn protects those who fear Him. (Psalm 33:18) Psalm 46:2 assures us, "Therefore we will not fear, Even though the earth be removed, And though the mountains be carried into the midst of the sea."

Harmful fears, on the other hand, drive us to lunacy and they come from evil when you least expect it. They are primarily driven by the wicked enemy. (Psalm 55:3-5) We do have one assurance from the Lord, "I will give peace in the land, and you shall lie down, and none will make you afraid; I will rid the land of evil beasts, and the sword will not go through your land." (Leviticus 26:6)

One root cause of fear is real, that is when we are outnumbered, but here we need to remember, Emmanuel, which means, God is with us. "When you go out to battle against your enemies, and see horses and chariots and people more numerous than you, do not be afraid of them; for the Lord your God is with you, who brought you up from the land of Egypt." (Deuteronomy 20:1)

There is also the fear of authority. For instance, we learn that Samuel was so afraid of Eli's authority that he could not bear to tell Eli about the judgment the Lord had just delivered on his household. (I Samuel 3:15) There are some who live in perpetual fear, even when things are going well in their lives. They say to themselves, "It is not going to last." Such negative expectations often translate into reality because as a man thinks in his heart so is he. (Proverbs 23:7) They live in perpetual slavery to the fear of failure and death. Hebrews 2:14-16 captures this perfectly:

> "Inasmuch then as the children have partaken of flesh and blood, He Himself likewise shared in the same, that through death He might destroy him who had the power of death, that is, the devil, [15] and release those who through fear of death were all their lifetime subject to bondage. [16] For indeed He does not give aid to angels, but He does give aid to the seed of Abraham."

Many people choose to avoid fear by not climbing their mountains to confront their fear of heights, forgetting that avoidance feeds our fears. When you avoid difficult routes to ascend the summit, you complicate your journey and you may miss the experience you might have gained from it. When we face our fears, even in baby steps, small increments, the fear gradually decreases as we expose them to the light of the gospel of Christ. Fear's hold on us is greatly diminished.

As Cloud and Townsend point out, we can internalize negative thoughts such as meanness and hatred, just as we can internalize positive ones like love and the fear of the Lord. [3] For instance, to overcome the fear of failure and self-doubt, we need to gain courage, apply ourselves diligently, gain skills and face every task with confidence trusting in the Lord.

Our spirit and mind often operate like an inerasable video or DVD recorder with a huge memory disc which can easily burn fears into our subconscious. Past fears are stored away in a temporary file in a place that is easily retrievable and accessible upon the slightest demand. However, the disc rarely contains the eventual outcome of our fears.

You may be scared of big black wolves which you have never seen in real life but continue to scare you, because of a bad movie you watched a long time ago. When fear grips you, the fact that the big black wolves were never real will not be part of the playback.

One of the things God assures us when we are born again is that He will make us new creatures and that "old things are passed away". (II Corinthians 5:17) To overcome such fears, we need to get information. Much of fear is steeped in ignorance. Read the Word of God, pray and seek counsel. Expose it to the light of Christ. Above all, the more you fear God, the less you fear men, things, spirits, darkness, heights and situations.

We can also gain a lot of confidence in the counsel of people of faith. We need the support and love that our team or community brings. In my job as defense counsel, I have had to counsel many couples going through serious emotional turmoil. I usually make it abundantly clear that the legal system can only go so far. I encourage them to seek counsel from their church leaders, respected community leaders or experienced family members. Many of them do follow up and a section of my office wall is laden with thank you cards from those whose relationships received a boost after following my advice.

It is important that we do not cripple our lives with the fear of fear. Courage is not the absence of fear but the presence of divinely inspired courage. We need to understand that some fears are normal. The fear of the Lord, for example, is the beginning of wisdom. We need to subject our thoughts to Christ. Fears are mostly irrational thoughts that we need to cast out of our mind. "Casting down arguments and every high thing that exalts itself against the knowledge of God, bringing every thought into captivity to the obedience of Christ." (II Corinthians 10:5) This can only happen when we start trusting the Lord with all our hearts and stop leaning on our own understanding. (Proverbs 3:5-6)

In other words, have the faith of God. (Mark 11:22-24) When we have faith in God, we don't question the assignment He has set before us because we know faithful is He that calls you who will also do it. He will never give us an assignment beyond our ability. (I Thessalonians 5:24)

In climbing the mountain, we have to realize that we walk by faith (another reality) and not by sight (sensory perception). The only antidote to fear is faith. Fear isolates us from God's power, capability, provision and promise, while faith summons us to move forward in total reliance on the reality of God's tremendous power, capability, provision and promise. Faith operates in the realm of possibilities.

When we use our sight, we see gargantuan mountains of problems and hardship that we can barely traverse, but when we walk by faith, we walk over the mountain. Faith in God can move the reality of the mountain before us. Faith is the bridge that connects you from the valley of pain, suffering, hardship and problems to the realm of possibilities where your invisible expectations are realized with God's divine provision.

So we need to ask God for help in prayer, learn from those who have gone before us and experienced similar circumstances. Study, understand and memorize Bible verses dealing with fear, faith, hope and God's faithfulness. Face your fears gradually and assuredly. Take small baby steps as long as you keep pulling down strongholds. Remember, "God has not given us a spirit of fear but of power and of love and of a sound mind." (II Timothy 1:7)

To lift us to greater heights while we march to the mountaintop, we need endurance. To endure means to remain firm under hardship and suffering without yielding to destructive forces and influences. We need lots of endurance to traverse the space between the foothills and our mountaintop. Endurance is the bridge that links our promise and its fulfillment. Whatever God has promised you, if you endure with patience, He will surely make it come to pass.

The bridge of endurance has seven main pillars. The first pillar is anchored in the deep understanding of the will of God. You have to know that the mountain you are on is the one the Lord has called you to overcome. "For you have need of endurance, so that after you have done the will of God, you may receive the promise." (Hebrews 10:36) There are many people in the world today needlessly enduring difficulty while pursuing other people's dreams. You need endurance to carry out the will of God for you, so that you may receive the promise.

The second pillar is that you have to understand it is a sprint of faith and not a "rat race", so you cannot use worldly means to endure. A lot of athletes in today's sports scene use performance-enhancing drugs to boost their performance. God will not lower His standards because you won. He is interested in the process that gets you the victory as much as the victory itself. The ends do not justify the means with God. If He was in the business of lowering His standards, then Moses would have made it to the Promised Land. "Therefore we also, since we are surrounded by so great a cloud of witnesses, let us lay aside every weight, and the sin which so easily ensnares us, and let us run with endurance the race that is set before us." (Hebrews 12:1)

The third pillar is our need to learn to endure sound doctrine and instruction. "For the time will come when they will not endure sound doctrine, but according to their own desires, because they have itching ears, they will heap up for themselves teachers." (II Timothy 4:3) Sometimes on your journey to the mountaintop, your coach, mentor, pastor and parents may tell you things that will cut against the grain and rub you the wrong way. You must be prepared to endure "sound doctrine". The Word of God is the standard you must use to judge such instruction.

The fourth pillar is to endure hardship. Mountaineering is not a cake walk. You have to learn to endure hardship like a good soldier of Christ (II Timothy 2:3) by living a life of discipline and routine in order to build strong mental, physical and spiritual muscles that can withstand the pressure of the mountain climb. Our Sunday school pastor at Spokane Dream Center, Pastor Vince Martin, never ceases to emphasize the need to wake up early in the morning and praise God. Sometimes you have to wake up early to pray as well as fast.

The fifth pillar commands us to endure hostility as Christ did. (Hebrews 12:3-4) Christ endured rejection and contradiction from his own people and yet

He made it to the mountaintop. Understand that people will misunderstand you and your motives but you have to keep on keeping on.

The sixth pillar of endurance is that of temptation. We have to endure temptation. Temptation is any distraction that will lead you outside of the path God has designed to reach your mountaintop. On the way to your destination, you will encounter many diversions and diversionary tactics of the enemy to lure you away from the path set out for you by Christ. Every time you pass this pillar, you are immediately rewarded with a crown. "Blessed is the man who endures temptation; for when he has been approved, he will receive the crown of life which the Lord has promised to those who love Him." (James 1:12)

Finally, we need to endure to the end, because it is only those who endure to the end that shall be saved. (Matthew 24:13) It may appear from the above pillars that we have an onerous task, but compared to what we, the New Testament believers have in contrast to the children of Israel, it might not be so bad:

[18] For you have not come to the mountain that may be touched and that burned with fire, and to blackness and darkness and tempest, [19] and the sound of a trumpet and the voice of words, so that those who heard it begged that the word should not be spoken to them anymore. [20] (For they could not endure what was commanded: "And if so much as a beast touches the mountain, it shall be stoned or shot with an arrow." [21] And so terrifying was the sight that Moses said, "I am exceedingly afraid and trembling.")

[22] But you have come to Mount Zion and to the city of the living God, the heavenly Jerusalem, to an innumerable company of angels, [23] to the general assembly and church of the firstborn who are registered in heaven, to God the Judge of all, to the spirits of just men made perfect, [24] to Jesus the Mediator of the new covenant, and to the blood of sprinkling that speaks better things than that of Abel." (Hebrews 12:18-24)

We have got it made! So let's go boldly to the mountain promised by our God. He has rewards lined up for us if we make it. We are blessed to even be counted worthy to be among those who will receive His mercy and compassion as we endure till the end. "Indeed we count them blessed who endure. You have heard of the perseverance of Job and seen the end intended by the Lord – that the Lord is very compassionate and merciful." (James 5:11) Like David, let us rise and continue the journey with patience and endurance without any fear, knowing full well that the Lord is our light and salvation. "The Lord is my light and my salvation; whom shall I fear? The Lord is the strength of my life; of whom shall I be afraid?" (Psalm 27:1)

PRINCIPLES

1. Fears are unavoidable, whether it be the fear of failure or the fear of heights.

2. Until the reason for our fears is addressed, it will remain perpetually an elephant in the room, or better yet, an elephant on the mountain!

3. Fear is our natural emotional reaction to danger and problems.

4. Fear warns us of impending catastrophe, however irrational it may be.

5. Fear makes you forget all your preparation, testimony, and most importantly, your Source, God, who has called you to go and take on the giant.

6. Once you allow fear to paralyze you and take over your thought process, it directs you to expect the worst outcome as the only plausible result. It makes you forget the God factor.

7. The key to victory over fear is to be planted by the waters; we know that water symbolizes the presence of the Holy Spirit.

8. Numbing and negative fear by itself is not the original purpose of fear in our life.

9. Positive fear drives us away from danger and evil and draws us closer to God's kind love and affection which is a place of safety and security and saves our lives from perdition.

10. The fear of the Lord is the beginning of knowledge, but fools despise wisdom and instruction. (Proverbs 1:7)

11. The negative force of fear is evil and deleterious to our health and sanity.

12. We cease to take risks and act in faith when fear sets in.

13. The very idea of self-preservation which fear seeks to introduce in our lives is antithetical to the very life Christ wants us to live.

14. Christ said, "Whoever seeks to save his life will lose it, and whoever loses his life will preserve it." (Luke 17:33)

15. The key to understanding the better place to turn when fear comes is to first of all understand the important difference between healthy fear and harmful fear as examined through the lens of our everyday preparation and the Word of God.

16. Both healthy fear and harmful fear comes from our spirit.

17. Healthy fear, according to Isaiah 11:2, comes with the Spirit of knowledge, wisdom, understanding, counsel and might. It is called the fear of the Lord – a reverential fear.

18. Harmful fear, on the other hand, drives us to lunacy and it usually comes from evil when you least expect it. It is primarily driven by the wicked enemy. (Psalm 55:3-5)

19. There is also the fear of authority. (I Samuel 3:15)

20. Many people choose to avoid fear by not climbing their mountains to confront their fear of heights, forgetting that avoidance feeds our fears.

21. Our spirit and mind often operate like an inerasable video or DVD recorder with a huge memory disc which can easily burn fears into our subconscious.

22. God assures us that when we are born again, He will make us new creatures and that "old things are passed away". (II Corinthians 5:17)

23. To overcome fear we need to get information, much of fear is steeped in ignorance. Read the Word of God, pray and seek counsel.

24. Expose your fears to the light of Christ. Read the Word of God, pray and seek counsel from godly men.

25. To lift us to greater heights while we march to the mountaintop, we need endurance.

26. The bridge of endurance has seven main pillars: will of God, faith, sound doctrine/instruction, hardship, hostility, temptation and finality.

Discussion Guide

1. What are you afraid of?

2. Look at the rationality of your fears in the light of the Word of God.

3. Discuss your fears with godly men or women.

4. Why do we need to endure?

5. What do we need to endure?

6. What is the critical importance of endurance in winning the race?

CHAPTER TEN
PREMATURE CELEBRATION
AT THE BRINK OF VICTORY

Every mountain top is within reach if you just keep climbing.
— Barry Finlay [1]

The other thing that often happens at the midway point, or close to the summit, is that some folks start celebrating even when they still have a considerable distance to cover. They forget it is not over until it is over. They take their eyes and gaze away from Christ, forgetting He is the author and finisher of our faith. (Hebrews 12:2) How many times have you seen a football player who is about to make a touchdown start to celebrate before he gets to the end zone and is tackled by the defense or even the punter? Many of the world's best soccer players routinely lose their penalty kicks. In 1986 at Mexico's World Cup, the whole world was astonished when France's Michel Platini strolled casually on the field to take the penalty kick against Germany and missed the shot. This stuff happens when you take your eyes off the prize.

Here is some much needed advice to keep you on track as you get near the end zone of your mountainous challenge.

1. It's simple – throw away the GPS! You don't need it. Stop torturing yourself. Stop looking at your wristwatch every few seconds. Ignore the calendar. Stop calculating how many days left before your graduation and celebration at the summit. Even more dangerous, stop deluding yourself that where you are is all there is for you. That would be very dangerous. Yes, you have achieved something substantial and by all means, celebrate your testimony, but remember like the angel told Elijah, the only luxury you are allowed is to eat. "And the angel of the LORD came again the second time, and touched him, and said, "Arise and eat; because the journey is too great for thee. And he arose, and did eat and drink, and went in the strength of that meat forty days and forty nights unto Horeb, the mount of God." (I Kings 19:7-8)(KJV)

A while ago, my little brother came to me excited that he had completed the National Certificate in Education in Nigeria and needed some money to pay the school before obtaining his certificate. His boundless excitement about his accomplishment was evident. However, I looked at all the potential in him and did not see an elementary school teacher. I told him point blank that I did not believe I should give him the money to get the certificate. "I only agreed to pay your tuition to attend the college of education as a stop-gap measure. My hope was that in the process you would focus more seriously on life." He was downcast and did not like my response. My brother tried to get our Mom to convince me to change my mind and provide the funding for him. Instead, I replied, "I will pay for you to take the law school entrance exam."

Earlier, my brother had shared that becoming a lawyer was his life's ambition. I promised to pay for all his law school tuition if he was willing to pursue his life goal. He decided to take me up on my offer. Today he is one of the most successful lawyers in our home state in Nigeria.

If I had allowed him to settle for less than the best, he might never have realized his dream. The last time I was in Nigeria he told the church he pastors that he would never have realized his ambition if I had not insisted that he go to law school. While he was so busy celebrating his diploma in education, he lost sight of his overarching goal, which was to become a lawyer.

When we stay too long in a local relief or crevice, we forget the main reason we are on the mountain is to overcome it; be it a mountain of debt or affliction. Temporary relief without addressing the entire problem is shortsighted. Geographical and geological scientists define local relief as, "The vertical difference in elevation between the highest and lowest points of a land surface within a specified horizontal distance or in a limited area. Also known as a relative relief." [2]

Always remember that a relative relief may not necessarily translate to a permanent relief. The fact that your aunt or cousin helped you pay next month's interest on your loan does not mean the mountain of debt is no more. Thank God for small mercies but don't lose sight of your overarching goal: getting rid of or overcoming your mountain of debt. Our joy should be in the fact that He who has begun a good work in us will surely accomplish it in Jesus' name. "Being confident of this very thing, that he which hath begun a good work in you will perform it until the day of Jesus Christ." (Philippians 1:6)(KJV)

As I said earlier, it is of great importance that we celebrate small achievements and celebrate our testimony, giving glory to God. Yes, you need to give glory to God for every day you are clean and sober and every day your business makes some forward strides. Every day you meet your debt repayment obligations, every day you reach your goal and every day you fulfill your potential, always give thanks. It is just as important to look forward as you look back, giving thanksgiving to God.

We don't make God greater when we praise and worship Him. When we worship and praise Him, it helps us to see Him as greater than our problems. The greater we see God the smaller we see our problems. When we lift Christ's name up and magnify God, our problems diminish before us. All of a sudden, you realize that the mountain before you is smaller than God. Now is the time to go back to the Word of God and get as much information as you can about the way forward. Learn and draw lessons from past experiences, from the successful to the debacle. It becomes easier to handle future hardships when you understand how you got yourself to that hard spot. It will surely make a big difference.

2. Keep the faith and keep your head. You are not here by your power. Willpower can only get you a little way. You are where you are by the grace of God Almighty. Usually when I teach at the discipleship house, many of the disciples who are clean and sober after completing their one month lockdown, get excited and think they know it all. Many often leave our program at this point because they think they can make it. Some who have never been sober for all their adult years suddenly become overconfident forgetting that it is faith in God that moves mountains and not faith in the flesh.

I agree that the instructions and the rules need to be relaxed after nine months, but relaxing enforcement of the rules does not mean abandoning the principles that have helped you surmount all the dangerous cliffs you have overcome. In fact, as I explained to some of the disciples, the discipleship program will be judged successful when the graduates, in their lives after graduation, begin to voluntarily enforce the rules and curfew that sustained them during the program.

The next stage is for you to start the necessary self-discipline that will make you function with little or no supervision for the rest of your life. Stay away from compromising positions. The Bible says flee all appearance of evil. (I Thessalonians 5:22) Some folks use a moment of respite from the grind of life to gorge themselves on what they have missed. They throw caution to the wind and start going back to the same neighborhood where God has just delivered them. Some refuse to do restitution and get rid of the ties to their past. Before you know it, if they were addicted to drinking or drugs they start out with something as legal as cigarettes that they quit years ago and then gradually slide back into using drugs again.

I often tell the disciples at our discipleship programs a story that Pastor Patrick Mejeidu of the Redeemed Christian Church of God, Grace Sanctuary, Lagos, Nigeria, once told us at a church workers' meeting several years ago. I still remember the outline of this sad story, even though the details are becoming a little fuzzy. It is the story of a Christian whose only problem was an addiction to smoking a pipe. When he gave his life to Christ he decided to quit the habit, and by the grace of God, within six months he stopped smoking it completely. However, he forgot to get rid of the pipe and kept it on top of a cabinet in his bedroom.

One night, he was having difficulty sleeping and kept tossing back and forth in bed. Suddenly he looked up and saw the pipe. He picked it up and started reminiscing about how he used to smoke. As he remained focused on his past, he remembered how difficult it was to get the money to support his habit; he even resorted to selling his wife's property!

When he could not afford a lighter, he borrowed a lighter from the neighbor. With the pipe in his hands, he suddenly realized there was some residue inside. Immediately he thought of his old neighbor and their time together. Walking down the street, the man found his neighbor outside smoking. The neighbor was surprised to see him at that time of the night, knowing that he was now a born-again Christian.

He replied, "Don't worry. I'm just remembering "the good old days"." Quickly he forgot that there was nothing good in the old days.

"Can I borrow your lighter?"

His neighbor handed over the lighter and he lit the pipe. Quickly, he picked up his old habit. In less than six months, he died of bronchitis and lung cancer. My prayer is that your story will be different, in Jesus' name.

3. You must be ready to accept the fact that the rest of the journey may not necessarily be as easy as the hike to the present spot. Accept the fact that the last half of the climb may not look like the first half. Things will not always go as planned. You will always face different situations and new devils. If you accept that the only constant in your life is Christ, your journey will be a lot easier. The reality is that you will have both moments of excitement and times of dryness. You have to learn to celebrate God in everything. You have to learn to live with different realities. The good thing is you will always find comfort in Christ and the solutions to your problems on a daily basis if you learn to trust Him. The various realities and challenges you are going to face will never take God by surprise. He sees the end from the beginning and He knows your every circumstance.

Faith is about being consistent in your walk with Christ for the rest of your life. We lose focus when we turn away from our faith in Christ and start focusing on the problem. What will help us in our travails is an unyielding desire to trust and obey the Lord. The more of God we see in our walk with Christ, the more quickly our besetting mountainous problems recede behind us.

What often happens is that we turn our gaze on the enemy. We want revenge and when we don't get it immediately we get mad, we get angry. Prophet Habakkuk's prayer in Habakkuk 3 has been one of the main pillars of inspiration to me while writing this book. Over the years, it has often been a source of inspiration in my daily walk with the Lord. God has used this passage/prayer over and over again to save me from depression.

In this prayer, Habakkuk starts out by acknowledging the sovereign power and brilliance of God. He says that he has heard about the testimonies of God and that the earth is filled with His praise. He recounts how God shatters the everlasting mountains, while onward swept the raging waters. (Habakkuk 3:6,10) (NLT) His glory on Mount Paran (Sinai) is such that the sun and the moon stood still. But by verse 16, the same Holy One who in His anger remembered His mercy (Habakkuk 3:2-3) (NLT) is the One the prophet is now praying to that God would strike the people who invaded his land. There is no doubt that Habakkuk was justifiably bitter against his Babylonian captors, so he schemes to use the power of God to avenge his enemies. But thank God for His mercy.

He suddenly remembers that a sad state does not change God. What moves God is faith, trust and obedience to His word. So he exclaims, "Even though the fig trees have no blossoms, and there are no grapes on the vine; even though the olive crop fails, and the fields lie empty and barren; even though the flocks die in the fields, and the cattle barns are empty, yet I will rejoice in the Lord! I will be joyful in the God of my salvation! The Sovereign Lord is my strength! He makes me as surefooted as a deer and brings me safely over the mountains." (Habakkuk 3:17-19) (NLT)

This is a remarkable change. We need to realize that we are where we are by His grace. Our resolute determined purpose should be the realization that when all is gone, God is not gone. As Matthew Henry aptly states, "Joy in God is never out of season, nay, it is in a special manner seasonable when we meet with losses and crosses in the world, that it may then appear that our hearts are not set upon these things, nor our happiness bound up in them." [3] The earlier we realize that our current circumstances will not define our concrete conclusion, the easier it is for us to rejoice in the God of our salvation. Like the three Hebrew children, Shadrach, Meshach and Abednego, we need to trust in our God in the midst of the perils of our life. Our love for Christ should never be tied to His blessings but by His very essence, God is love! Temporary victory or setbacks should never change our trust and faith in Him.

An interesting incident occurred while I was putting the finishing touches on this book. One of my clients, someone the court often calls my success story, came to court with a motion asking to be relieved of the counseling requirement of his probation. The judge asked him why he sought such relief and he stated that he was feeling good. He was at the top of his life. My client believed he had been saved from a life of addiction and didn't think he should listen to the words of a 27-year-old counselor who did not have the same life experience.

Pride is fatal as it often lures the prideful to celebrate at the brink of victory.

The probation officer asked me if we could speak to him together. As soon as we came together, he wouldn't let us start or complete a sentence. He kept talking about how well he was doing and why he didn't need any more counseling. Verbally he attacked his counselor, vehemently running him down. I sensed he was going through what I call the "halfway to the summit crisis".

It was also evident that this brother loved God and was genuine in his belief that he was doing well. This is someone who had been homeless for a long time until the Lord took him literally out of the miry clay. I sensed the weapon the enemy was using against him was pride. It was shocking to him when I told him, "This is the most vulnerable moment of your life."

The enemy was using the very achievement and testimony God gave him to puff him up with pride. I told him, "Submit to your counselor no matter how young the person is." He listened to me and reflected on it and agreed to withdraw his motion.

In I John 2:16, the Bible speaks of the three snares the enemy frequently uses against us, the lust of the flesh, the lust of the eyes and the pride of life. The most subtle of this troika is the pride of life. It is dangerous because most often you will feel justified to ogle your own achievement. Our culture even encourages blowing or tooting your own horn, even when it is only a broken horn and all that is coming from it are discordant tunes no one is interested in hearing. The pride of life is fatal as it ultimately leads to your downfall when you least expect it.

Pride is also fatal as it often lures the proud to celebrate at the brink of victory. The key to overcoming such temptation is to ascribe all our achievements to the One who makes it possible – Jesus Christ, our Lord, and to look unto Him, who is the author and finisher of our faith to take us safely to the summit. The prophet, Habakkuk, understood this well as he immediately ascribed all to God. He said in Habakkuk 3:19, "The Sovereign Lord is my strength! He will make me as surefooted as a deer, and brings me safely over the mountains." (NLT)

PRINCIPLES

1. When we stay too long in a local relief or crevice, we forget the main reason we are on the mountain is to overcome it.

2. Always remember that a relative relief may not necessarily translate to a permanent relief.

3. Celebrate small achievements and celebrate our testimony, giving glory to God but don't lose sight of the overarching objective: Overcome.

4. The greater we see God, the less we see our problems.

5. It becomes easier to handle future hardships when you understand how you got yourself to that hard spot.

6. Keep the faith and keep your head.

7. Accept the fact that the last half of the climb may not look like the first half.

8. The various realities and challenges you are going to face will never take God by surprise.

9. Our culture encourages us to blow or toot our own horn, even when it is half broken and no one is interested in listening to the discordant tunes.

10. Pride is often fatal as it lures the prideful to celebrate at the brink of victory.

11. Remember God is the one that will make you strong and bring you safely over the mountain.

DISCUSSION GUIDE

1. Where are you with the dream God has given you?

2. Are you prematurely celebrating or lingering on the way up?

3. How do you see God in your daily grind in life? Do you see God in your challenges?

4. Are you so familiar with your present circumstances that you have resigned yourself to the status quo?

CHAPTER ELEVEN
THE MOUNTAINTOP EXPERIENCE

If you don't climb the mountain you can't see the view.
– Anon [1]

Congratulations! You made it to the top of your mountain. You endured hardship, suffered tremendous pain, overcame debilitating circumstances, fought herds of naysayers, confronted self and the sneering doubt of others, conquered hunger and deprivation to get to the summit. Now that you are here, you need to take in the view, relax and enjoy. Celebrate and enjoy your achievements, but remember how you got here. Give all the glory and praise to the one who protected you through the valley of the shadow of death, the jagged edges of disastrous weather, the desert of hunger and "the forest of one thousand demons". It is the Lord that has kept you through thick and thin, safe, sound and healthy even when many with much greater strength than yours were falling down and dashing their heads against the rock. He protected you from "the snares of the fowler" and "the perilous pestilence". (Psalm 91:3-4)

The importance of success in life and ministry cannot be shrugged away. The desire and hunger to succeed was put in us by our Creator and to Him we owe whatever success we may achieve. One quote attributed to Thomas Carlyle says, "the great law of culture is: Let each become all that he was created capable of being; expand if possible, to his full growth; and show himself at length in his own shape and stature, be these what they may." [2]

You have to remember, though, that this mountaintop is your temporary platform where God has placed you. It could be a marital mountaintop with an awesome wife that cares for you or a financial mountaintop where you are able to pay all your bills and provide for your family. It can even be a spiritual mountaintop of awesome revelation that will change your ministry, your church and your congregation. Always remember the assignment. Do not get carried away by the glitz and the glamour forgetting the very reason why you came to the mountain in the first place.

Conversely, there are others who strive desperately to climb the corporate ladder of success in either secular or ministry work, only to realize when they get there that it is nothing but an empty mountaintop view. They look around and find it difficult to recognize those around them. They have left their wife, children and family behind in the valley and lowlands in their inordinate ambition/quest to get up the mountain of "me, myself and I". A place they have not been called by God to climb has consumed them, probably because they saw others successful in the same position, forgetting each of us has a different assignment. The siren call of grandiose achievement has driven them berserk.

I once had a meeting with a good family friend in Nigeria, who by all means of wealth measurement had it all. When I started applauding his monumental achievement, he looked at me and sighed. "I wish I could trade all of my wealth for success in my marriage." He continued, "I wish I had not neglected my children when they needed me the most."

This is why (as we stated in earlier chapters) at every point in our quest to reach the summit a large dose of self-examination is sorely needed. We need to take time, slow down, look around, take stock of our position and check our priorities and motives in the light of Christ.

At one time in my career, I was nominated by my mentor for the Washington State Bar Association Leadership Institute. It was the opportunity of a lifetime. I was honored to be among the elite members of the Bar Association and community leaders in our state once every month when we traveled to various Bar Association meetings and leadership seminars. At the end of the program, I had an opportunity to move to Seattle or Olympia to advance my legal career but I balked. First of all, I sought the face of the Lord and He showed me that I had not completed my assignment in Spokane. Second, I looked at my children and I could not bear to uproot them from their friends, classmates and church friends for a quest that involved better pay for me. Third, if I took a busy law firm position I would find it extremely difficult to spend time with my family not to mention my ministry. I would then revert back to the life I used to live in Nigeria when I wouldn't see my wife for at least a week or two because of my law firm assignments. Finally, I discovered that even though I would be making more money at a busy law firm, I likely would not be able to make an impact on people's lives as I do now working as a public defender. I decided to stay in Spokane. I am glad I didn't take the bait, even though I enjoyed my time as a Fellow of the Washington State Bar Association Leadership Institute. The friends I made then are still there for me and they remain part of my professional network that I frequently call upon when I need to get something done in our state.

The desire and hunger to succeed was put in us by our Creator and to Him we owe whatever success we may achieve.

Nevertheless, God is a God of mercy, even when we miss the mark. Wherever you may find yourself, all you need to do is call on Him who is able to bring life back to your dream. You may have lost your children but God can restore whatever was stolen from you. The Bible says, "And the Lord restored Job's losses when he prayed for his friends." (Job 42:10a) Indeed the Lord gave Job twice as much as he had before.

Your mountaintop platform could be the space and the place where your gifts, talents, and skills make room for you. It is however important to warn you that one of the most vulnerable moments in life is the immediate moment of victory when you feel on top of the world. David learned a bitter lesson about this in II Samuel 11.

To fully understand the background to this story one has to start from II Samuel10:16-19, where we learn that David defeated Hadadezer, king of Zobah. In I Chronicles 18:1-3, we see the importance of this victory when the Bible states, "And David defeated Hadadezer king of Zobah as far as Hamath, as he went to establish his power by the River Euphrates"; with this conquest David (who may have found out from the sons of Issachar who had understanding of the times and knew what Israel ought to do) effectively brought to pass God's promise to Abraham, "To your descendants I have given this land, from the river of Egypt to the great river Euphrates." (Genesis 15:18)

The story of David and Bathsheba reminds us how quickly leadership can falter but yet find a pathway to redemption. In II Samuel 11:1, the Bible says, "It happened in the spring of the year, at the time when kings go out to battle, that David sent Joab and his servants with him and all Israel; and they destroyed the people of Ammon and besieged Rabbah. But David remained at Jerusalem." He sent others to go to battle at a time when all the other kings went to battle. His victory over Hadadezer apparently went to his head.

Indeed, Israel's territory at this time had increased by more than one hundredfold from the small kingdom he inherited from Saul. He chose to stay on top of the mountain he had just surmounted instead of getting ready for more challenges. King David got comfortable with yesterday's victory and forgot that getting to the mountain is one thing, sustaining and maintaining your hold upon the mountain is a completely different "kettle of fish".

You can delegate many things in life, but the one thing you cannot delegate is your divine assignment. The mountain God assigned for you can only be accomplished by you.

An example of another leader who tried to dodge his duties is Moses. In the burning bush story, Moses gave all kinds of excuses on why he should not be sent. Finally, when God probably couldn't stand his whining anymore, He sent help for Moses through his brother, Aaron. "Now the Lord had said to Aaron, "Go out into the wilderness to meet Moses." So Aaron traveled to the mountain of God, where he found Moses and greeted him warmly." (Exodus 4:27) (NLT) God will always send help your way and bless you with gifted people, but you must take the lead in the battle to defend and establish dominion over your mountain. You can't outsource your divine assignment. In Exodus 7:1, "Then the Lord said to Moses, "Pay close attention to this. I will make you seem like God to Pharaoh. Your brother, Aaron, will be your prophet, he will speak for you." (NLT) Even though Aaron initially took the lead, Moses started speaking directly to Pharaoh what the Lord commanded beginning in Exodus 8:9. Whatever happened to his stammering? Stop putting your impediment before God. He will use you just as you are. Come to Him today!

Going back to the story of David and Beersheba, the consequences of David's sloppiness were not only scandalous but also proved to be fatal. "Then it happened one evening that David arose from his bed and walked on the roof of the King's house. And from the roof he saw a woman bathing, and the woman was very beautiful to behold." (II Samuel 11:2) It is fitting and apropos for us that the Bible states that David arose from bed and walked on the roof. We may not know for certain why he was walking on the roof, but ancient kings often walked the roof of their palace to luxuriate and revel in the majesty of their kingdom. They forgot that it is God who sets up kings and no one can assume a position of authority without the approval of God. We see the downfall of another king in the same circumstances in Daniel 4:28-32:

> All this came upon King Nebuchadnezzar. [29] At the end of the twelve months he was walking about the royal palace of Babylon. [30] The king spoke, saying, "Is not this great Babylon, that I have built for a royal dwelling by my mighty power and for the honor of my majesty?" [31] While the word was still in the king's mouth, a voice fell from heaven: "King Nebuchadnezzar, to you it is spoken: the kingdom has departed from you! [32] And they shall drive you from men, and your dwelling shall be with the beasts of the field. They shall make you eat grass like oxen; and seven times shall pass over you, until you know that the Most High rules in the kingdom of men, and gives it to whomever He chooses.

David may not be exactly like King Nebuchadnezzar, but he was also on the roof of the palace when he saw a woman. Somehow he got power drunk, thinking he could always have whatever he desired and do whatever he pleased even if that thing belonged to someone else.

At the mountaintop of rest, covetousness often surreptitiously creeps in. There is a point at which our mountainous achievement can sometimes goad us into thinking we are above all and that we can get away with everything and anything. Forgetting that God is the one that makes all things possible and without Him we are nothing.

I believe pride and hubris played a significant role in David's adultery with Bathsheba and his subsequent murder of her husband, Uriah. David paid a hefty price for resting and carousing when he should have been up and doing. He paid a heftier price for his sins. One of his sons committed incest while another one took revenge by killing that son and then tried to seize the throne from David. One only need read Psalm 51 to see David's emotional turmoil after the man of God, Nathan, exposed his shenanigans. That is a warning to all of us to be cautious in choosing to rest on the mountain we've just conquered instead of proceeding to the next assignment after catching our breath.

Christ gives us a clear pattern to employ in responding to the enemy in such moments. Jesus Christ, our Lord and Savior, shows us how to overcome the inevitable temptations that come from enjoying the thrills of accomplishment after a successful mountaintop experience. In Matthew 4:1-17 as well as Luke 4:1-15, the Bible says, Jesus being filled with the Holy Spirit was led by the Spirit into the wilderness where He fasted for forty days and was tempted by the devil. The Bible records that the devil took Him up on an exceedingly high mountain and showed Him all the kingdoms of the world and their

> *Every successful completion of a divine assignment in our life should actually bring us into the presence of God, where we will see God in all His holiness and then enjoy His rest.*

glory as well as the pinnacle of the temple. The first is for political power and the second is priestly power. What was his question to Jesus? "All these things I will give you if you will fall down and worship me."

Jesus said to him, "Get behind me, Satan! For it is written, you shall worship the Lord your God and Him only you shall serve."

The Bible says the devil left Him, until an opportune time, and "behold angels came and ministered to Him."

Immediately, the Bible records that Christ did not sit down to enjoy the view of the mountain forever. He returned in the power of the Spirit and taught in the synagogue. From that time on, Jesus began to preach and to say, "Repent, for the kingdom of heaven is at hand."

We discover immediately that He began to select His disciples and in chapter 5 of the book of Matthew, He took them up on a mountain and preached the Sermon on the Mount, which we now call, the Beatitudes. If we can overcome the temptation and pride that comes from standing on top of the mountain and come back down to lead others up the mountain, our ministry will be fulfilled.

This is not to say that God deplores rest, not at all. In fact, God himself rested on the seventh day after creation. Seven, of course, is the number of perfection, and until we are perfect, we should limit our celebration of every achievement to the minimum.

Every successful completion of a divine assignment in our life should actually bring us into the presence of God, where we will see God in all His holiness and then enjoy His rest. And as we behold the beauty of His holiness it will contrast with our "filthy rags". (Isaiah 64:6) A mountaintop experience also makes us see the emptiness of the world. (I John 2:15-17)

The beautiful thing is that a moment in the presence of God on His Holy Mountain will open our eyes to the innumerable angels on assignment for us.

There we will also discover that God's true rest can only come to us when we abide in Him and do His will. (Matthew 11:28) We will then discover the true purpose for our lives as Paul did in Acts 26:13-16. The awesome thing about dwelling in His presence is that like Moses, a little bit of His glory will rub off on us. (Exodus 34:29-30) Even though we may not notice it, others will notice it.

Our first task on the mountaintop is to worship God and bow down in adoration to the King of kings. It is often at the summit of such mountain that the good Lord reveals the next assignment and promotes His generals. As we learned earlier in this chapter, it is one thing to conquer one solitary mountain by achieving success in business, sports or ministry. It is another thing to be successful in your primary assignment, which is your family.

As I've reiterated throughout this book, my message is not a call to vain glory. It is not a call to pursue a "me, myself and I" agenda to the exclusion of all others or to the exclusion of caring and showing affection for God's people. Stewart Green reminds us of the danger of self glory among 'modern-day mountaineers' and their lack of care for others in their selfish bid to achieve a personal record, when he wrote about the tragic story of British climber, David Sharp, as follows:

"There are many tragic stories like that of British climber David Sharp, who sat down under an overhang 1,500 feet below the summit on May 15, 2006 after successfully climbing Mount Everest. He was extremely tired after a long summit day and began freezing in place as he sat there. As many as 40 climbers trudged past him, believing him already dead or not wanting to rescue him, on one of the coldest nights that spring. A party passed him at 1 in the morning, saw he was breathing still, but continued on to the summit since they didn't feel they could evacuate him. Sharp continued freezing through the night and the next morning. he had no gloves on. He was undoubtedly hypoxic from lack of oxygen and probably had no idea where he was nor felt any pain."

"Sharp's death created a huge storm of controversy over what was considered the callous attitude of the many climbers who passed the dying man yet made no attempt to rescue him, feeling that it would jeopardize their own ascent of the mountain. Sir Edmund Hillary, who made the first ascent of Mount Everest in 1953, said it was unacceptable to leave another climber to die. Hillary told a New Zealand newspaper: "I think the whole attitude towards climbing Mount Everest has become rather horrifying. The people just want to get to the top. It was wrong if there was a man suffering altitude problems and was huddled under a rock, just to lift your hat, say good morning and pass on by." [3]

As I worked on this book, the Lord led me to reflect on the state of the church in America. Even though this book is meant to awaken our dreams and passion to fulfill our potential in Christ, that potential must seek to advance Christ's influence in our nation and throughout the world. This inevitably took me to a vision many Christians in America have forgotten. I think it is imperative that we reproduce the summary here for clarity:

"In 1975, Bill Bright, founder of Campus Crusade, and Loren Cunningham, founder of Youth with a Mission (YWAM), had lunch together in Colorado. God simultaneously gave each of these change agents a message to give to the other. During that same timeframe, Francis Schaeffer was given a similar message. That message was that if we are to impact any nation for Jesus Christ, then we would have to affect the seven spheres, or mountains of society, that are the pillars of any society. These seven mountains are business, government, media, arts and entertainment, education, the family and religion. There are many subgroups under these main categories."

"About a month later, the Lord showed Francis Schaeffer the same thing. In essence, God was telling these three change agents where the battlefield was. It was here where culture would be won or lost. Their assignment was to raise up change agents to scale the mountains and to help a new generation of change agents understand the larger story." [4]

At the time when these men of God received this vision, American broadcast networks started their live broadcasts with prayer and schools started the day with prayer as well. Billy Graham frequently had live broadcasts of evangelistic crusades on American broadcast networks. One cannot recall the last time any major broadcast network covered a gospel-related activity in recent years. And yet we wonder why the culture of the world is dominant in today's America.

The church leaders at the time either chose to ignore the call or dismiss the vision as improbable. Those who heard the cry stood up and did the best they could. Sadly, the church is now paying dearly for the neglect of that era. The only mountain the church occupies with regularity, since that time, is the mountain of religion. Even that is being squeezed daily given the decline in church attendance. For us to see true revival and for the gospel of Christ to have an influence on our society and the law, we need to encourage believers to seek to maximize their potential in climbing every one of these mountains. It is not too late.

More importantly, the church needs to raise awareness about this vision and encourage Christians, individually and corporately, to live the life of Christ while replicating their successful mountaintop experiences in religious spheres into other areas of their lives such as business, government, media, arts and entertainment, education, and the family, for not only a moment in time, but frequently. After all, success in the Household of God is measured in terms of its generational impact on society. (Jeremiah 35:1-6) All of which leads us to the next call...Legacy.

PRINCIPLES

1. Celebrate and enjoy your achievements, but remember how you got to the summit.

2. Give all the glory and praise to the one who protected you through the valley of the shadow of death, the jagged edges of disastrous weather, the desert of hunger and "the forest of one thousand demons".

3. The desire and hunger to succeed was put in us by our Creator and to Him we owe whatever success we may achieve.

4. You have to remember, though, that this mountaintop is a temporary platform where God has placed you.

5. Do not get carried away by the glitz and the glamour forgetting the very reason why you came to the mountain in the first place.

6. Some strive desperately to climb the corporate ladder of success in either secular or ministry work, only to realize when they get there that it is nothing but an empty mountaintop view.

7. They have left their wife, children and family behind in the lowlands, and now there is no one to enjoy their achievement with them.

8. At every point in our quest to reach the summit, a large dose of self-examination is sorely needed.

9. We need to take time, slow down, look around, take stock of our position and check our priorities and motives in the light of Christ.

10. God is a God of mercy. Even when we miss the mark and call on Him, He is able to make us whole again and bring us safely over the mountain of our dreams.

11. Our first task on the mountaintop is to worship God and bow down in adoration to the King of kings.

12. Your mountaintop platform could be the space and the place where your gifts, talents, and skills make room for you.

13. At the mountaintop of rest, covetousness, arrogance and pride et al. often surreptitiously creep in.

14. There is a sense in which our mountainous achievement can sometimes goad us into thinking we are above all and that we can get away with everything and anything.

15. Christ gives us a clear pattern to employ in responding to the enemy in such moments.

16. Jesus Christ, our Lord and Savior, shows us how to overcome the inevitable temptations that come from enjoying the thrill of accomplishment after a successful mountaintop experience.

17. The Bible records that Christ did not sit down to enjoy the view of the mountain forever. He returned in the power of the Spirit and taught in the synagogue.

18. If we can overcome the temptation and pride that comes from standing on top of the mountain and come back down to lead others up the mountain, our ministry will be fulfilled.

19. Every successful completion of a divine assignment in our life should actually bring us into the presence of God, where we will see God in all His holiness and then enjoy His rest.

20. The beautiful thing is that a moment in the presence of God on His Holy Mountain will open our eyes to the innumerable angels on assignment for us.

21. Our first task on the mountaintop is to worship God and bow down in adoration to the King of kings.

22. It is often at the summit of the mountain of achievement that the good Lord reveals the next assignment and promotes His generals.

23. This is not a call to pursue a "me, myself and I" agenda but a call for caring and showing affection for God's people.

24. Even though this book is meant to awaken our dreams and passion to fulfill our potential in Christ, that potential must seek to advance Christ's influence in our nation and throughout the world.

25. Success in the Household of God is measured in terms of its generational impact on society. (Jeremiah 35:1-6)

DISCUSSION GUIDE

1. Share your recent testimonies with one another.

2. Have you had time to take stock of your life recently? Do it now.

3. Can you challenge each other about times in your past when you prematurely or excessively celebrated before the final victory?

4. How often do you get your family involved in your mountain climb?

5. Are you given to sitting on your laurels?

6. Survey the state of the church in your country/region and think about where you fit in to advance the gospel of Christ.

"Celebrate what you've accomplished, but raise the bar a little higher each time you succeed."

— *Mia Hamm*

CHAPTER TWELVE
THE LEGACY

If all you're about is winning; it's not really worth it.
I'm after things that last.
— Keli McGregor [1]

I bet when you read the title of this chapter, you thought I was going to be talking about naming one mountain or another after yourself as a legacy to your achievement in conquering it. Or maybe, you are someone who has built a company from scratch and plans on putting your stamp on it by naming it after yourself? Is that what you thought this chapter was going to be about? Well, it is not. A legacy is not just about naming mountains, buildings, corporations and charity centers after architects, founders and explorers. It is about the impact you make on the sands of time. In other words, what you leave behind in terms of character, integrity, dedication, faith and leadership to name a few.

Macmillan Online Dictionary defines enduring legacy as "something that someone has achieved that continues to exist after they stop working or die." [2] This surmises that as climbers, for our work to stand the test of time we need to have an achievement which will outlive us or our time on the mountaintop. The word "enduring" is derived from the word "endure" which means to remain firm under hardship/suffering without yielding to destructive forces and influence.

One morning, I asked my friend, the rock climber, about this topic because I wanted him to give me a comparable analogy of those within the climbing community that have left an enduring legacy. He took a deep breath and smiled, and then said, "Within the climbing community, there are people who spend tons of money buying anchors and tools to create routes. Some make it easy, others make it difficult. I always believe that we should set routes as if we are making it for beginners. I have lots of respect for those who do that. They make it safe for others. If it is too simple for you, just adjust it and ignore the simple routes." [3]

A climbing route is a path by which a climber reaches the top of the mountain, rock or ice wall. In the early days of mountaineering, climbers got to the top by whatever means they could find. Very little information is available about how they did it. As explorers tried more difficult summits, it became necessary to have safer routes for those who would later make their ascent up the mountain.

It became common practice for the first climber to choose a name for the route. Often the names incorporated a pun or reflected precisely where the routes went. The first climbers often spend a considerable number of hours and money setting routes. They build a lasting legacy on the route to the summit that often outlives them.

There are many legendary climbers who have paved the way for others. By establishing routes where none existed before, they make it possible for beginners to find their bearings. Their name and notoriety may not necessarily be plastered all over the rocks and the mountains but their thankless efforts live long in the minds of those who will later ascend the mountain.

As author, Nelson Henderson, opines, "The true meaning of life is to plant trees, under whose shade you do not expect to sit." [4] A true lasting legacy goes beyond personal benefit and personal success to adding value to the lives of others. By touching and impacting the lives of others around us, and by replicating in words and deeds the virtues that brought us to the mountaintop, we can create value beyond our reach so those we teach and impact may pass it on to others on and on, ad infinitum.

Chances are that many route setters never get the kudos for impacting other people's lives, but that does not stop them from doing the job. As the writer of Hebrews states, "And all these, having obtained a good testimony through faith, did not receive the promise. God having provided something better for us, that they should not be made perfect apart from us. Therefore, we also since we are surrounded by so great a cloud of witnesses, let us lay aside every weight and the sin which so easily ensnares us and let us run with endurance the race that is set before us." (Hebrews 11:39-12:1) We must always live our life as if it depends on making others better and inspiring those around us, even those we may never meet or know; knowing that God who brought us to the mountain and guides our steps will guide theirs, too.

A lasting legacy does not necessarily mean we are number one in everything we do. In fact, most people make a more lasting impact when they are in a supporting role. One good example of a man with an enduring legacy in a supporting role is John the Baptist. He was a rabbi before Christ was ever called a rabbi. He had disciples before Christ, and in fact, the majority of Christ's disciples were first his and yet he released them to Christ. He was settled in his assignment. John the Baptist knew his calling and had no conflict about his assignment. Here is what he said when some folks came to inform him that Christ was taking over his job.

And they came to John and said to him, "Rabbi, He who was with you beyond the Jordan, to whom you have testified – behold, He is baptizing, and all are coming to Him!"

John answered and said, "A man can receive nothing unless it has been given to him from heaven. You yourselves bear me witness, that I said, 'I am not the Christ,' but, 'I have been sent before Him.' He who has the bride is the bridegroom; but the friend of the bridegroom, who stands and hears him, rejoices greatly because of the bridegroom's voice. Therefore this joy of mine is fulfilled. He must increase, but I must decrease." (John 3:26-30)

This is the testimony of a man settled in his assignment and comfortable in his own skin. No wonder Jesus testified of him as follows, "For I say to you, among those born of women there is not a greater prophet than John the Baptist; but he who is least in the kingdom of God is greater than he." (Luke 7:28) What an awesome legacy! We know that those of us in Christ, and with the added anointing of the Holy Spirit, actually stand to build a better legacy than John the Baptist. There is no doubt that having an opportunity to pass on your successful mountaintop experience and inspiring others to undertake the same is the hallmark of an enduring legacy.

In fact, the measure of success in the kingdom of God is determined by the multi-generational impact of our work. In Genesis 18:17-19, the Lord said the reason He could not hide anything from Abraham is, "For I know him, that he will command his children and his household after him, and they shall keep the way of the Lord, to do justice and judgment; that the Lord may bring upon Abraham that which he hath spoken of him." (Genesis 18:19) (KJV) As Bishop Tudor Bismark rightly pointed out, the reason why we could say, "God of Abraham, Isaac and Jacob" is because Abraham invested in his children and grandchildren. [5]

Abraham was 100 years when Sarah (90 years old) gave birth to Isaac. (Genesis 21:5) Sarah died at the age of 127 years, and at that time, Abraham was 137. For three years, Isaac mourned the loss of his mother, before Abraham asked his servant to look for a wife for him. Isaac married Rebekah at the age of 40 years. (Genesis 25:20) Isaac was 60 years old when Rebekah bore the twins – Esau and Jacob. (Genesis 25:26) In Genesis 25:7, we learn Abraham was 175 years old when he died. This meant Abraham spent 15 years with Jacob and Esau reminding them of the promise and covenant he had with God. This, in a way, is part of the reason why Abraham became the Father of Faith along with the fact that he believed God in every situation.

> *"The true meaning of life is to plant trees, under whose shade you do not expect to sit." – Nelson Henderson*

A more interesting example of a character-building legacy story is the Rechabites in Jeremiah 35:1-19. God instructed Jeremiah to test the whole house of the Rechabites to see if they would break the oath of their father, Jonadab, the son of Rechab, that he made with the Lord not to drink wine along with his household. They passed the test and refused to break the oath. The Lord speaking through Jeremiah the prophet promised to keep the legacy of Jonadab forever because of their faithfulness to their oath in following the legacy of their forefathers:

> [18] And Jeremiah said unto the house of the Rechabites, Thus saith the Lord of hosts, the God of Israel; Because ye have obeyed the commandment of Jonadab your father, and kept all his precepts, and done according unto all that he hath commanded you:

[19] Therefore thus saith the Lord of hosts, the God of Israel; Jonadab the son of Rechab shall not want a man to stand before me forever. (KJV)

Our society today is given to instant gratification. We want the glory and the gold, and we want it right away, even at the expense of future generations. We incur huge debt to finance our luxury and then pass it along to our grandchildren to pay the bill. The thought of leaving a legacy for future generations is never in our calculations. A call to the mountain summit of influence and divine revival is long overdue and we need to humble ourselves and bear our cross daily, following the footsteps of Christ who has called us to the summit of faith and denial. When we die to self and gain Christ, we build a lasting legacy like Jonadab, son of Rechab. Hear the call to the Body of Christ, "Arise!"

PRINCIPLES

1. Legacy is what you leave behind in terms of character, integrity, dedication, faith and leadership to mention but a few.

2. The word "enduring" is derived from the word "endure" which means to remain firm under hardship/suffering without yielding to destructive forces and influence.

3. A climbing route is a path by which a climber reaches the top of the mountain, rock or ice wall.

4. First-time climbers often spend a considerable number of hours and money setting routes.

5. They build a lasting legacy on the route to the summit that often outlives them.

6. A true lasting legacy goes beyond personal success to adding value to the lives of others.

7. By touching and impacting the lives of others around us, and by replicating in words and deeds the virtues that brought us to the mountaintop, we can create value beyond our reach so those we teach and impact may pass it on to others.

8. A lasting legacy does not necessarily mean we are number one in everything we do. In fact, most people make a more lasting impact when they are in a supporting role.

9. The measure of success in the kingdom of God is determined by the multi-generational impact of our work.

10. When we die to self and gain Christ, we build a lasting legacy like Jonadab, son of Rechab.

DISCUSSION GUIDE

1. Discuss what legacy means to you and your group.

2. Do you have to be #1 to have a lasting legacy?

3. Discuss how you and your group can make a lasting impact on your home church, your community and your nation.

EPILOGUE

*May your dreams be larger than mountains and
may you have the courage to scale their summits.*
–Harley King [1]

As I conclude this book, I have found two stories particularly instructive, one is personal and the other is about the life of a legendary basketball player. The personal story is an incident that happened to me at my workplace. My two work colleagues called it a "teachable moment". At work, I am well-known for my belief in Christ. Often, my colleagues look at me as a representative of Christ, chiefly because I don't curse or threaten anyone. I remind them that I am just as human as everyone else but for the grace of God and the help of the Holy Spirit.

One morning, one of our female co-workers who was going through some difficult circumstances came to meet my next door colleague, looking for someone to unload on or just generally seeking advice and direction. My other colleague, who was also not having a good morning, summarily dismissed her out of his office.

I felt his curt statement about not having time for whining was too strident so I approached him and suggested he go to her and apologize. He immediately took my advice and went to her and apologized. Later that afternoon I was in her cubicle and our discussion drifted to her curt treatment by our colleague. I assured her that it would not happen again. Then I made the stupidest mistake of my life, I told her, "I asked him to apologize to you."

She said, "Really?"

I stupidly said, "Yes."

The following day as soon as I arrived at the office, my colleague, whose office is next to mine, called me and asked me to come over to his office because I was about to have a "teachable moment."

He said, "How does it feel to tell a guy to go and apologize, which I did, and then you go talk to the person I hurt and tell her, "by the way, I asked that guy to apologize."

I immediately realized the error of my ways and apologized to him profusely. It was an embarrassment of monumental proportions. I believe that Paul's lesson in I Corinthians 10:12 is very instructive, "Therefore let him who thinks he stands, take heed lest he fall." We might have climbed the tallest mountain and held aloft the banner of Christ but we still have to remember our walk with Christ is a daily walk. It is a walk of faith in the Son of God. It is only when we humble ourselves and submit to Christ that we can overcome.

The second story I found particularly poignant in drawing out the lessons of this book is the story of the legendary basketball star, Allen Iverson of Philadelphia 76ers fame. The Washingtonpost.com posted the story three years after his legendary NBA career ended. Allen is a man blessed by God with tremendous talent to play the game of basketball. Despite being only a 6-foot, 165-pound point guard, at the height of his game, he frequently embarrassed many defenders with his feints and twists on the way to the basketball hoop, both in college and the NBA.

At one point, his frame could barely hold his fame. But three years after his last NBA game, the spotlight shifted from his play to his flaws. [2] He personally attested to the fact that when he was playing the game, his God-given gifts and talents made room for him: "I put it in God's hand…I just understand that He helped me accomplish a lot of things in the NBA. I've done so many things that people thought that I couldn't do …" [3]

There is no doubt that God moved mountains for Allen to be among the best basketball players in the world. He blessed him with tremendous talents, a loving wife and family and a game he loved and cherished. Allen, however, never really contemplated that God wouldn't be moving every mountain all the time. He moved the mountain of his size and height so Allen could compete with others and climb, as well as conquer, other mountains in his life. Allen, however, could not see it.

> *The good thing for those of us in Christ Jesus is that our Savior assures us that He won't let us carry the pressure of this world alone.*

At the height of his game, he would either refuse to show up for practice with the team or practice with a hangover after a night out that included drugs and alcohol and carousing with women. He frequently skipped team functions and refused to obey the league's dress code. His response to a question in 2002 about missing workouts became iconic: "We're talking about practice." [4] The arrogance on the court would have been sufficient but he carried it home. He was an absentee husband and father.

Tawanna, his ex-wife, testified at their divorce proceedings that during their family vacation Iverson would very often abandon his family while they made plans without him. On one occasion, the Washington Post reporter states that Allen left his little children alone in a hotel room during a weekend at the water park and Tawanna had to pick them up at 2 a.m. with one of the kids still in her swimsuit. Tawanna was awarded custody of all the children after her testimony to the effect that she had "always thought that my kids needed their father… and what I've learned is that they don't need him if he's going to be that destructive in their lives." [5]

As he continued to succeed on the court, many people were willing to overlook his obvious flaws, teammates accepted all the hangovers during practice as his unique trademark, his family appeared at courtside with smiles on their faces, and the NBA also played along, at least "as long as his game was sharp – he was named MVP in 2001 and won four NBA scoring titles." [6] The rest of the public ignored all else as they only saw what they projected on him and that was the image of a man whose determination made him get the better of the giants.

But then the inevitable happened. Allen Iverson's body could no longer take the punishing and grueling task of practicing with a hangover after a night out, but he wouldn't let go of the alcohol and the carousing. Like Samson, he thought his mountain-moving faith would always be there, even in the absence of character. Kent Babb, the Washington Post reporter sums up the inevitable:

This is something most everyone but Iverson has accepted, and for years a question worried those closest to him: <u>What happens when the most important part of a man's identity, the beam supporting the other unstable matter, is no longer there?</u> [emphasis added] For the past three years, as Iverson chased an NBA comeback, his marriage fell apart and much of his fortune – he earned more than $150 million in salary alone during his career – dissolved. Now, those who once ignored past signals have recognized that basketball may have been the only thing holding Iverson's life together. "He has hit rock bottom, and he just hasn't accepted it yet," says former Philadelphia teammate Roshown McLeod. [7]

However, what the reporter missed is that the most important supporting beam of the unstable Iverson's life was not basketball as he could always play basketball albeit to a smaller audience. What he missed was God's grace which had sustained him with or without the gift, something he had taken for granted. His faith, like all faith, had to be supported by work. Work is practice and work is character.

As the writer of the Book of James stated, "For as the body without the spirit is dead, so faith without works is dead, also." (James 2:26) Allen Iverson had faith in his God-given talent, he even knew that God gave him the talent but in the end, his character and moral failing destroyed him. "What does it profit, my brethren, if someone says he has faith but does not have works? Can faith save him?" (James 2:14)

This is a poignant warning to us all. Yes, God moves mountains for us, but He also encourages us to walk in the reality of His Word. "For we are his workmanship, created in Christ Jesus unto good works, which God hath before ordained that we should walk in them." (Ephesians 2:10)

All hope is not lost for Iverson, he may still get his family back, and if he lives to the age of 55, he will be entitled to a staggering sum of $30 million from an endorsement deal put in escrow for him by Reebok. The sad reality, however, is that the money may again go the way the $70.9 million he got from his 1999 six-year NBA contract and the subsequent $76.7 million contract did unless he allows God to make and mold him and bring him up the upward climb to the mountain of strong moral character and faith.

Iverson, like every one of us, has to get a grip on reality that what gifts and talents, money and fame bring are not necessarily enough to assure peace and joy. We have to embrace the entire message of the giver of gifts, talents and money. He (God) is the one we need to trust and obey, (as the ancient hymn implores), for there is no other way to be happy in Jesus but to trust and obey.

The reality is the time to build that strong moral character is now. Iverson and all of us should not wait until God moves our mountains and casts them into the sea. Start climbing as you pray in faith for His will to come to pass in your life. We need to have a determined purpose to see the will of God come to pass in our lives whether He moves the mountain of hardship we are going through or not. As the prophet Habakkuk enthused, "Even though the fig trees have no blossoms, and there are no grapes on the vines; Even though the olive crop fails, and the fields lie empty and barren; Even though the flocks die in the fields, and the cattle barns are empty, yet I will rejoice in the Lord! I will be joyful in the God of my salvation! The Sovereign Lord is my strength! He will make me as surefooted as a deer, and brings me safely over the mountains." (Habakkuk 3:17-19) (NLT) The three Hebrew children, Shadrach, Meshach and Abednego said, "If it be so, our God whom we serve is able to deliver us from the burning fiery furnace, and he will deliver us out of thine hand, O king. But if not, be it known unto thee, O king, that we will not serve thy gods, nor worship the golden image which thou hast set up." (Daniel 3:17-18) (KJV) As Isaiah urged, our faith in God should make us set our face like a flint, trusting God in the face of every adversity.

The Lord GOD hath given me the tongue of the learned, that I should know how to speak a word in season to him that is weary: he wakeneth morning by morning, he wakeneth mine ear to hear as the learned. The Lord GOD hath opened mine ear, and I was not rebellious, neither turned away back. I gave my back to the smiters, and my cheeks to them that plucked off the hair: I hid not my face from shame and spitting. For the Lord GOD will help me; therefore shall I not be confounded: therefore have I set my face like a flint, and I know that I shall not be ashamed. He is near that justifieth me; who will contend with me? let us stand together: who is mine adversary? let him come near to me. Behold, the Lord GOD will help me; who is he that shall condemn me? lo, they all shall wax old as a garment; the moth shall eat them up. Who is among you that feareth the LORD, that obeyeth the voice of his servant, that walketh in darkness, and hath no light? let him trust in the name of the LORD, and stay upon his God. Behold, all ye that kindle a fire, that compass yourselves about with sparks: walk in the light of your fire, and in the sparks that ye have kindled. (Isaiah 50:4-11a) (KJV)

What we need to do is trust in the name of the Lord and stand upon the Word of our Lord and Savior and He will give us a "future and a hope" in Him. "For I know the thoughts that I think toward you, saith the Lord, thoughts of peace, and not of evil, to give you an expected end." (Jeremiah 29:11) (KJV) Look up and see Jesus. There are no better words to end this book than the immortal poem of Henry Wadsworth Longfellow, *The Cross of Snow*.

> In the long, sleepless watches of the night,
> A gentle face – the face of one long dead –
> Looks at me from the wall, where round its head
> The night-lamp casts a halo of pale light.
> Here in this room she died, and soul more white
> Never through martyrdom of fire was led
> To its repose; nor can in books be read
> The legend of a life more benedight.
> There is a mountain in the distant West
> That, sun-defying, in its deep ravines
> Displays a cross of snow upon its side.
> Such is the cross I wear upon my breast
> These eighteen years, through all the changing scenes
> And seasons, changeless since the day she died. [8]

You may not have lost a wife, like Mr. Longfellow, but whatever you've lost, the glow of the cross of Christ is there for you to wear on your chest. It will sustain you. Christ is our hope. More importantly, we need to understand that the mountain quest is not an end in itself.

Mark Obmascik writing about his three-year journey to summit the Fourteeners peaks in Colorado said, "After each of these peaks, I returned home with a little more pride and skill and stamina, plus the humility to realize that nothing I could do on a mountain would ever be as hard or rewarding as staying home for the past three years with our three kids." [9]

We might have climbed the tallest mountain and held aloft the banner of Christ but we still have to remember our walk with Christ is a daily walk.

One of his co-climbers also reflects, "I have found that having some money and the chance to pretty much do what you want is more daunting than one might think – a sort of be careful what you wish for, because Working for the Man, so to speak, is an easy excuse for not living out your dreams. When faced with the midlife realities of what are my dreams and do I have the guts to go after them with no financial excuses – well, that is a lot more pressure than one would think." [10]

The good thing for those of us in Christ Jesus is that our Savior assures us that He won't let us carry the pressure of this world alone. In fact, He said we should cast our burdens and yoke on Him. He in turn will give us a yoke and burden that are light and easy. He said, "Come unto me, all ye that labor and are heavy laden, and I will give you rest. Take my yoke upon you, and learn of me; for I am meek and lowly in heart: and ye shall find rest unto your souls. For my yoke is easy, and my burden is light." (Matthew 11:28-30) (KJV)

I don't know what you are going through right now, it might be a light or heavy yoke. I do know that Christ's promise is open and available to you, all you need to do is call on Him and He will help you. If you have never given your life to Christ, I urge you to yield to Him today. Even if you think you are righteous, you still need Him. The Bible says, "For all have sinned and fall short of the glory of God." (Romans 3:23) In fact, if we say, we are without sin there is no truth in us (I John 1:8) but if we confess our sins, He is faithful and just to forgive us our sins and to cleanse us from all unrighteousness. (I John 1:9)

Next, we need to acknowledge Christ as the Son of God. (I John 2:23) In return, Christ gives us a new life. We become a new creature and old things will pass away, all things will become new. (II Corinthians 5:17)

The same message that was made available to Allen Iverson is available to all of us if we would humble ourselves and set aside our mountain summit achievement and come to Him with a humble heart. True riches, everlasting peace and eternal joy can only be found in Christ, embrace Him today. He alone is the one who will make us and bring us safely over the mountains of our lives.

PRINCIPLES

1. We might have climbed the tallest mountain and held aloft the banner of Christ but we still have to remember our walk with Christ is a daily walk.

2. It is a walk of faith in the Son of God. It is only when we humble ourselves and submit to Christ that we can overcome till the end.

3. Yes, God moves mountains for us, but He also encourages us to walk in the reality of His Word.

4. We need to have a determined purpose to see the will of God come to pass in our lives whether He moves the mountains of hardship in our lives or not.

5. What we need to do is trust in the name of the Lord and stand upon the Word of our Lord and Savior and He will give us a "future and a hope" in Him.

6. When we acknowledge Christ as the Son of God, (I John 2:23) He (Christ) in turn gives us a new life.

7. True riches, everlasting peace and eternal joy are only available (abundantly) in Christ.

DISCUSSION GUIDE

1. Discuss with your group what true riches mean in the light of the Word of God.

2. How can we arrive safely at the summit?

3. Why do we need Him to make us strong and bring us over the mountain?

NOTES

INSPIRATION

1. This scripture passage, Habakkuk 3:1-4, 17-19 has often been a veritable source of strength and encouragement to us at Spokane Dream Center and to me personally. Several years ago, at an early morning prayer meeting prior to the Sunday service (frequently attended by some of the pastors) we were led by the Spirit of the Lord to pray to God every verse of Habakkuk 3. At the end of the meeting, we were astounded to find, as Habakkuk did, that the "sovereign Lord is our strength". Recently, I preached an impromptu message on this chapter at a Sunday morning service. Throughout the preparation, writing and research for this book, this scripture passage gave me hope and strength to safely summit the mountain.

PREFACE

1. Henry Wadsworth Longfellow, *"The Cross of Snow"* Public Domain. "Henry Wadsworth Longfellow's wife died tragically when an ember from the fireplace caught her dress on fire and burnt her so badly that she died a few days later. Longfellow tried to put out the fire, and it is said that his face was so badly disfigured that he grew the familiar long beard to hide the scars. Eighteen years later he was looking at a book with pictures of the Far West and the mountains when he came across a picture much like the one reproduced here. The poem that resulted is "The Cross of Snow," one of his most poignant and touching sonnets". Retrieved from http://english.emory.edu/classes/paintings&poems/longfellow.html

2. John Muir *"The Wilderness World of John Muir"*, a selection from his collected works, Edited by Edwin Way Teale, 2001, p. 318, Mariners Book/Houghton Mifflin Books. www.HoughtonMifflinbooks.com

3. Ibid. (Muir, p.321). Pilgrims of the Vertical: Yosemite Rock

4. Joseph E. Taylor, *"Pilgrims Climbers and Nature at Risk"* p. 233, Cambridge, MA: Harvard University Publishers, 2010. Print.

5. Mark Obmascik *"Halfway to Heaven"* p. 57, published by Atria Books May 12, 2009.

PROLOGUE

1. Henry, Matthew. "Commentary on Genesis 19." . Blue Letter Bible. 1 Mar 1996.2013. Accessed 19 Aug 2013 from <http:// www.blueletterbible.org/ commentaries/comm_view.cfm?
AuthorID=4&contentID=646&commInfo=5&topic=Genesis >
2. Guzik, David, Bible Commentaries. Quoted with permission from http:// www.enduringword.com/commentaries/0119.htm Accessed 8/19/2013.

PART ONE

CHAPTER ONE

1. Obsmascik, Mark: *Halfway to Heaven*, p. 146, published by Atria Books May 12, 2009.
2. PBS: Nova Online Adventure, "Lost on Everest" retrieved 7/19/2013 from http://www.pbs.org/wgbh/nova/everest/lost/mystery/voices.html last updated November 2000.
3. Onoda: *My 30 Year War*, Blue jacket Books, October 1999.
4. Merriam-Webster.com Accessed online 8/19/2013 from http://www.merriam-webster.com/dictionary/mountain
5. Patterson, Richard D. "Five Star Mountains" Quoted with permission from Bible.org. Copyright ©1996-2006 Bible.org, reprinted with permission. Accessed online 8/19/2013 from https://bible.org/article/five-star-mountains
6. Holman Bible Dictionary. Butler, Bradley S. Editor. Entry for Mountain. Published by Broadman & Holman, 1991. Used by permission of Broadman & Holman. Accessed 8/19/2013 from http://www.studylight.org/dic/hbd/view.cgi?number=T4425

CHAPTER TWO

1. Muir, John, Accessed 8/19/2013 from http://www.goodreads.com/quotes/tag/mountains
2. Patterson, Richard D. "Five Star Mountains" Quoted with permission from Bible.org. Copyright ©1996-2006 Bible.org, reprinted with permission. Accessed online 8/19/2013 from https://bible.org/article/five-star-mountains
3. Ibid.
4. Summitpost.org. "A short introduction on the history of mountain guiding" Accessed online 8/19/2013 from http://www.summitpost.org/a-short-introduction-on-the-history-of-mountain-guiding/696433

5. Ibid.

6. Muir, John. *Our National Parks*. Boston: Houghton, Mifflin and Company, 1901; Electronic Version Accessed at http://wadsworth.cengage.com/history_d/templates/student_resources/0030724791_ayers/sources/ch20/20.4.muir.html

7. Holman Bible Dictionary. Butler, Bradley S. Editor. Entry for Mountain. Published by Broadman & Holman, 1991. Used by permission of Broadman & Holman. Accessed 8/19/2013 from http://www.studylight.org/dic/hbd/view.cgi?number=T4425

8. Patterson, Richard D. "Five Star Mountains" Quoted with permission from Bible.org. Copyright ©1996-2006 Bible.org, reprinted with permission. Accessed online 8/19/2013 from https://bible.org/article/five-star-mountains

9. Paprocki, Joe. "Paprocki Answers: What is the significance of mountains in the Bible?" Accessed 8/19/2013 and reproduced with permission from: http://bustedhalo.com/questionbox/what-is-the-significance-of-mountains-in-the-bible

Additional Note: Joe Paprocki, D.Min, is a National Consultant for Faith Formation at Loyola Press in Chicago. He has over 30 years of experience in pastoral ministry in the Archdiocese of Chicago. Joe is the author of numerous books on pastoral ministry and catechesis, including The Bible Blueprint, Living the Mass, and bestsellers, The Catechist's Toolbox and A Well-Built Faith (all from Loyola Press).

10. Wood, Bryant G. "What Do Mt. Horeb, The Mountain of God, Mt. Paran and Mt. Seir Have to Do with Mt. Sinai?" Published online Biblearchaeology.org. Accessed on 7/22/2013 from http://www.biblearchaeology.org/post/2008/11/What-Do-Mt-Horeb2c-The-Mountain-of-God2c-Mt-Paran-and-Mt-Seir-Have-to-Do-with-Mt-Sinai.aspx#Article

11. Smith, Chuck. "Hebrews 12-13." The Word for Today. Blue Letter Bible. 1 Jun 2005 Accessed 19 Aug 2013 from <http://www.blueletterbible.org/commentaries/comm_view.cfm?AuthorID=1&contentID=7254&commInfo=25&topic=Hebrews >

12. Guzik, David, Bible Commentaries. Quoted with permission from http://www.enduringword.com/commentaries/0224.htm

13. LawofLiberty.com. *Mounts of the Bible*. Quoted with permission from Lawofliberty.com. Accessed online 7/22/2013 from http://lawofliberty.com/sermons/Resources/mountsofthebible.pdf

14. Stedman, R. "Exodus Design for Deliverance" Online Bible Commentaries. Quoted with permission from www.RayStedman.org. Copyright © 2010 by Ray Stedman Ministries. Accessed 7/22/2013 from http://www.raystedman.org/bible-overview/adventuring/exodus-design-for-deliverance

15. Ibid.

16. Wesley, John. "John Wesley's Explanatory Notes", Public Domain Available. Accessed online 7/22/2013 from: http://www.christnotes.org/commentary.

php?com=wes&b=2&c=32

17. Meyer, Frederick M. *"Elijah and the Secret of his Power"*. Public Domain Available Accessed online 7/22/2013 from http://www.baptistbiblebelievers. com/BooksoftheBible/ElijahandtheSecretofhisPowerFBMeyer/tabid/309/ Default.aspx

18. Ibid.

19. Ibid.

20. Jamieson, Robert; A.R. Fausset; and David Brown. "Commentary on Deuteronomy 34." Public Domain Available. Published online by Blue Letter Bible. 19 Feb 2000. 2013. Accessed online 20 Aug 2013. <http://www. blueletterbible.org/commentaries/comm_view.cfm?AuthorID=7&contentID= 2068&commInfo=6&topic=Deuteronomy >

21. Munroe, Myles "Understanding God's Plan"; online sermon accessed on YouTube 7/22/2013 from http://www.youtube.com/watch?v=cpT9O_FIO_s

22. LawofLiberty.com. *Mounts of the Bible*. Quoted with permission from Lawofliberty.com. Accessed online 7/22/2013 from http://lawofliberty.com/ sermons/Resources/mountsofthebible.pdf

23. Ibid.

24. Patterson, Richard D. "Five Star Mountains" Quoted with permission from Bible.org. Copyright ©1996-2006 Bible.org, reprinted with permission. Accessed online 8/19/2013 from https://bible.org/article/five-star-mountains

CHAPTER THREE

1. Kintz, Jarod. Quotes from, *American Association for the Advancement of Aardvarks Presents: Dear Natalie* Accessed online 8/20/2013 from http://www.goodreads. com/quotes/tag/mountains

2. Van Wart, Montgomery. *Dynamics of Leadership in Public Service*, p. 23, Publisher, M.E. Sharpe, 2005. ISBN, 0765629364

3. Adeboye, Enoch. Process of Mountain Climbers. Accessed online 8/20/2013 from http://eaadeboye.com/audios/?_pg=4

4. Patterson, Richard D. "Five Star Mountains" Quoted with permission from Bible.org. Copyright ©1996-2006 Bible.org, reprinted with permission. Accessed online 8/19/2013 from https://bible.org/article/five-star-mountains

5. Ibid.

6. LawofLiberty.com. *Mounts of the Bible*. Quoted with permission from Lawofliberty.com. Accessed online 7/22/2013 from http://lawofliberty.com/ sermons/Resources/mountsofthebible.pdf

7. Ibid.

8. Adeboye, Enoch. Process of Mountain Climbers. Transcribed and Accessed online 8/20/2013 from http://eaadeboye.com/audios/?_pg=4

9. Patterson, Richard D. "Five Star Mountains" Quoted with permission from

Bible.org. Copyright ©1996-2006 Bible.org, reprinted with permission. Accessed online 8/19/2013 from https://bible.org/article/five-star-mountains

10. Ibid.

11. Alden, R.L. "Jordan" The Zondervan Pictorial Encyclopedia of the Bible. Ed. Merrill C. Tenney. 5 Vols. Grand Rapids: Zondervan Publishing House, 1976.

12. LawofLiberty.com. *Mounts of the Bible*. Kyle Campbell. Quoted with permission from Lawofliberty.com. Accessed online 7/22/2013 from http://lawofliberty.com/sermons/Resources/mountsofthebible.pdf

13. Ibid.

14. Ibid.

PART TWO

CHAPTER FOUR

1. Mensah, Otabil. "Mountain Moving Faith" Online sermon last accessed 7/22/2013 from http://www.youtube.com/watch?v=fZiU9jB6D_w

2. Adeboye, Enoch. Process of Mountain Climbers. Transcribed and Accessed online 8/20/2013 from http://eaadeboye.com/audios/?_pg=4

3. Ibid.

CHAPTER FIVE

1. Obsmascik, Mark: *Halfway to Heaven*, p. 86, published by Atria Books May 12, 2009.

2. Hartman, Henry. Online quotes accessed 7/5/2013 from http://thinkexist.com/quotes/henry_hartman/

3. Horst, Eric J. *How to Climb: Flash Training*, p. 84, How to Climb Series, 1994, Publisher: Falcon Guides, ISBN 9780934641777

4. Green, Stewart, "Death on Mount Everest: How Climbers Die on Mount Everest" Quoted with Permission and Retrieved 7/5/20013 from About.com

5. Obmascik, Mark. *Halfway to Heaven: My White-knuckled - and Knuckleheaded - Quest for the Rocky Mountain High* p. 57. 2009. Publisher: FreePress

6. Green, Stewart: Death on Mount Everest; quoted with permission and retrieved online 7/5/2013 from www.About.com

7. Obmascik, Mark. *Halfway to Heaven: My White-knuckled - and Knuckleheaded - Quest for the Rocky Mountain High* p. 56-57. 2009. Publisher: FreePress

8. Horst, Eric J. *How to Climb: Flash Training*, p. 84, How to Climb Series, 1994, Publisher: Falcon Guides, ISBN 9780934641777

9. Ibid.

10. Darroch, David & Alice. *Feeding on His Faithfulness*. Published 2006. www.XulonPress.com

1. Obmascik, Mark. *Halfway to Heaven: My White-knuckled - and Knuckleheaded - Quest for the Rocky Mountain High* p. 56-58. 2009. Publisher: FreePress

2. Mathis, B. Livestrong.com "Ten Essentials Items for Mountain Climbing" Accessed online 7/22/2013 http://www.livestrong.com/article/507171-ten-essential-items-for-mountain-climbing/

3. Otabil, Mensah "Go Borrow Vessel", CD available for purchase online at https://jesushousedc.org/store/Go_Borrow_Vessels___CD-details.aspx

4. Mathis, B. Livestrong.com "Ten Essentials Items for Mountain Climbing" Accessed online 7/22/2013 http://www.livestrong.com/article/507171-ten-essential-items-for-mountain-climbing/

5. Green, Stewart: Death on Mount Everest; quoted with permission and accessed online 7/5/2013 from www.About.com

6. Mathis, B. Livestrong.com "Ten Essentials Items for Mountain Climbing" Accessed online 7/22/2013 http://www.livestrong.com/article/507171-ten-essential-items-for-mountain-climbing/

7. Tozer, A. W., Fellowship of the Burning Heart, p. 80. Transcribed Sermons. Edited by James Snyder. Pure God Classic Series, 2006. Publisher: Bridge Logos publishing

8. Ashimolowo, Matthew Online sermon "Standing on the Promises of God", online podcast accessed 8/26/2013 from https://itunes.apple.com/us/podcast/matthew-ashimolowo-audio-podcast/id357535538

9. Spurgeon, C. H. "Spiritual Warfare: A Believer's Life, p.166. Compiled and Edited by Robert E. Hall. Publisher: Emerald Books, 1996

10. Mathis, B. Livestrong.com "Ten Essentials Items for Mountain Climbing" Accessed online 7/22/2013 http://www.livestrong.com/article/507171-ten-essential-items-for-mountain-climbing/

11. Henry, Matthew. Commentaries on Ephesians. Accessed online 8/26/2013 from http://www.biblegateway.com/resources/matthew-henry/Ephesians

12. Mathis, B. Livestrong.com "Ten Essentials Items for Mountain Climbing" Accessed online 7/22/2013 http://www.livestrong.com/article/507171-ten-essential-items-for-mountain-climbing/

13. Obmascik, Mark. *Halfway to Heaven: My White-knuckled - and Knuckleheaded - Quest for the Rocky Mountain High* p. 166. 2009. Publisher: FreePress

14. Mathis, B. Livestrong.com "Ten Essentials Items for Mountain Climbing" Accessed online 7/22/2013 http://www.livestrong.com/article/507171-ten-essential-items-for-mountain-climbing/

15. Stewart M. Green & Ian Spencer-Green, "Knack Rock Climbing: A Beginners Guide: From the Gym to the Rock" Knack: Make it Easy Series, p. 62. Publisher: Globe Pequot Press. 2010

16. Ibid.

17. Ford, James. Online sermon podcast: Moody Radio: Treasured Truth. Accessed online 7/22/2013 from http://www.moodyaudio.com/radio/treasured-truth

18. Mathis, B. Livestrong.com *"Ten Essentials Items for Mountain Climbing"* Accessed online 7/22/2013 http://www.livestrong.com/article/507171-ten-essential-items-for-mountain-climbing/

19. Ibid.

CHAPTER SEVEN

1. Obmascik, Mark. *Halfway to Heaven: My White-knuckled - and Knuckleheaded - Quest for the Rocky Mountain High* p. 231. 2009. Publisher: FreePress

2. Ibid.

3. Ibid. p.233

4. Cloud, Henry and Thompson, John *"Safe People: How to Find Relationship That are Good for you and Avoid Those that Aren't"* p. 27, Publisher, Zondervan, 1996

5. Green, Stewart. John Bachar: American Rock Climbing Icon. 2009. Posted online and quoted with permission from About.com. Accessed 8/26/2013 from http://climbing.about.com/od/topclimbers/p/John-Bachar-American-Rock-Climbing-Icon.htm

6. Cloud, Henry and Thompson, John *"Safe People: How to Find Relationship That are Good for you and Avoid Those that Aren't"* p. 26, Publisher: Zondervan, 1996

7. Ibid. P.29

8. Author's Interview with Brian Raymond April 24, 2013

9. Ibid.

10. Cloud & Townsend, *"Safe People: How to Find Relationships that are Good for You and Those that Aren't"* p. 113, Zondervan, 1996

11. Dungy, Tony. *The Mentor Leader*, p. 70, Tyndale House -Publisher, 2013

12. Ibid., p. 139

PART THREE

CHAPTER EIGHT

1. Dungy, Tony. *The Mentor Leader*, p. 57, Tyndale House -Publisher, 2013

2. Cloud, Henry and Thompson, John *"Safe People: How to Find Relationship That are Good for you and Avoid Those that Aren't"* p. 88, Publisher, Zondervan, 1996

3. Bismark, Tudor. Online message "Establishing Dominion" Accessed 8/26/2013 from http://www.ctab.org/sermons/guests/establishing-dominion-by-tudor-bismark/

4. Pascal, Blaise, Quote retrieved 8/26/2013 from http://www.brainyquote.com/quotes/quotes/b/blaisepasc159856.html

5. Burke, Edmund. Quote retrieved 7/22/2013 from http://www.goodreads. com/quotes/90880-nobody-made-a-greater-mistake-than-he-who-did-nothing

CHAPTER NINE

1. Obmascik, Mark. *Halfway to Heaven: My White-knuckled - and Knuckleheaded - Quest for the Rocky Mountain High* p. 231. 2009. Publisher: FreePress
2. Roberts, David "No strings attached" published online April 11, 2011. Outside Magazine. Accessed 8/26/2013 from http://www.outsideonline.com/outdoor-adventure/climbing/rock-climbing/No-Strings-Attached.html
3. Cloud, Henry and Thompson, John *"Safe People: How to Find Relationship That are Good for you and Avoid Those that Aren't"* Publisher, Zondervan, 1996

CHAPTER TEN

1. Finlay, Barry "Kilimanjaro and Beyond" quote retrieved 8/26/13 from http://www.goodreads.com/quotes/tag/mountains
2. McGraw-Hill Dictionary of Scientific & Technical Terms, 6E, Copyright © 2003 by The McGraw-Hill Companies, Inc.
3. Henry, Matthew Commentaries on Habakkuk. Accessed 8/26/2013 from http://www.biblegateway.com/resources/matthew-henry/Hab.3.16-Hab.3.19

CHAPTER ELEVEN

1. From a poster found at the Mullan Road Elementary School Gym, Spokane, Washington
2. From the series Great Ideas of Western Man, online retrieved 7/19/2013 from http://greatideas.omeka.net/exhibits/show/exhibit
3. Green, Stewart "Death on Mount Everest". Quoted and reproduced here with permission from About.com. Accessed 7/22/2013 from http://climbing.about.com/od/mountainclimbing/a/Death-On-Mount-Everest.htm
4. Hillman, OS. Quotes used with permission of Reclaim7mountains.com. Accessed 7/9/10 from http://www.reclaim7mountains.com/

CHAPTER 12

1. Quote attributed to the late Keli McGregor, former president Colorado Rockies Baseball Club, by Rev. Peter Morin, pastor of Faith Lutheran Church, during the funeral oration for Keli. The pastor retold this quote to extol McGregor's values and how they related to running his organization – Colorado Rockies. Morin said McGregor always kept cards in his pocket, to write things Morin said in church down for future reference. "[Keli] said, 'You know, Peter, there are 29 losers

every year in baseball,'" Morin related. "'Don't get me wrong – I want to win.' He was a competitive man, for sure. "But he said, 'If all you're about is winning, it's not really worth it.' It had to be about things that last." Quote excerpted from article titled "McGregor celebrated in moving ceremony" by Harding, Thomas. Posted online at MLB.com 4/25/2010. Accessed 8/26/13 from http://mlb. mlb.com/news/article.jsp?ymd=20100425&content_id=9568090&vkey=news_col&fext=.jsp&c_id=col

2. Macmillandictionary.com. Accessed 8/26/2013 from http://www.macmillandictionary.com/dictionary/british/legacy

3. Author's conversation with Brian Raymond, April 23, 2013

4. Henderson, Nelson. Quotes accessed online at goodreads.com 8/26/2013 from http://www.goodreads.com/quotes/102763-the-true-meaning-of-life-is-to-plant-trees-under

5. Bismark, Tudor. Online message "Establishing Dominion" Accessed 8/26/2013 from http://www.ctab.org/sermons/guests/establishing-dominion-by-tudor-bismark/

EPILOGUE

1. King, Harley. Quotes accessed 8/26/13 from http://www.goodreads.com/quotes/531208-may-your-dreams-be-larger-than-mountains-and-may-you

2. Baab, Kent. "Allen Iverson, NBA icon, struggles with life after basketball" published online April 19, 2013 by The Washingtonpost Co. Accessed April 23, 2012 from http://articles.washingtonpost.com/2013-04-19/sports/38666036_1_allen-iverson-sixers-nba-s

3. Ibid.

4. Ibid.

5. Ibid.

6. Ibid.

7. Ibid.

8. Henry Wadsworth Longfellow, *"The Cross of Snow"* Public Domain. Posted online and accessed 6/20/13 from http://english.emory.edu/classes/paintings&poems/longfellow.html

9. Obmascik, Mark. *Halfway to Heaven: My White-knuckled - and Knuckleheaded - Quest for the Rocky Mountain High* p. 153. 2009. Publisher: FreePress

10. Ibid.

ACKNOWLEDGEMENTS

Bernard of Chartres used to say that we are like dwarfs on the shoulders of giants, so that we can see more than they, and things at a greater distance, not by virtue of any sharpness of sight on our part, or any physical distinction, but because we are carried high and raised up by their giant size.
– John of Salisbury (Metalogicion, 1159)

As apparent from the numerous quotes of the scriptures, sermons and contemporary authors on mountaineering, rock climbing, mountain-moving faith and the process of mountain climbing, I owe so many people for helping me on this journey. In fact, they are too numerous to mention.

First of all, I am grateful to Almighty God, the giver and Source of life. Nothing could be achieved in life without Him. For by Him all things were made and without Him nothing was made that was made. He is the light of men.

I also owe Bishop (Dr.) Mensah Otabil, of International Central Gospel Church and Pastor Enoch Adejare Adeboye, the General Overseer of the Redeemed Christian Church of God Worldwide. They both brought out something that challenged me to write this book. I made copious references to their sermons in this book particularly their respective sermons on "Mountain Moving Faith" and "The Process of Mountain Climbing".

Other secular authors on mountain and rock climbing also helped me a great deal, particularly Mark Obmascik. The others I have listed in the Bibliography.

My lovely sweetheart, Olamide Adewale, your unwavering support and passion for the things of God remains a source of encouragement to me and our children.

Samuel, Deborah, David, Daniel and Sarah, my lovely children, thank you for listening to me as I instruct you in the ways of the Lord.

All my pastors, Pastor Patrick Mejeidu, Pastor Eloka Uzodike, Pastor Ghandi Olaoye, Pastor Muyiwa Karunwi, Pastor Samuel Sorinmade, Pastors David and Alice Darroch, thank you for providing the forum that allows me to use my gifts and encourage God's people.

I also wish to thank other family members, church members, all past and present disciples of Spokane Dream Center's Discipleship programs (the laboratory for this book), as well as my editor, Barbara Hollace and my printer, Gray Dog Press, led by Russ Davis and his team. I am grateful. Thank you all.

ABOUT THE AUTHOR

Francis A. Adewale is an assistant public defender, pastor, civil rights activist and public administrator. Born in Ilesa in southwest Nigeria, he graduated from Nigerian Law School in 1992 and practiced for eight years with one of Africa's top ten law firms in Lagos, Nigeria. He was also a lay pastor with one of Africa's fastest growing churches, Redeemed Christian Church of God.

In 1999, Francis and his family emigrated to the United States and in 2005, he became a U.S. citizen. Also in 2005, he was ordained as a pastor by Pastors David and Alice Darroch of Spokane Dream Center. For over 10 years, he has been involved with teaching at the Dream Center in their Bible School and Men's and Women's Discipleship Programs.

He is a proud member of the Washington State Bar Association, Nigerian Bar Association and American Bar Association. In 2012, he completed his Master's degree in Public Administration with honors.

Mr. Adewale is a regular speaker at many forums in the Inland Northwest of the United States as well as in Nigeria. In addition to his work with the Public Defender's office, he holds a free limited legal clinic at Spokane Dream Center and also assists minority businesses in the Spokane area.

His heart for service is also evidenced by his work as a director with Spokane's Refugee Connections, a nonprofit organization that connects refugees to resources within the Spokane region as well as a nonprofit public interest law firm – PMCI, patterned after Spokane Center for Justice, in his homeland of Nigeria. The Center focuses on five main areas: civil rights, discrimination, government accountability, poverty and the environment.

Over the Mountains is his first book and reflects his passion to see believers fulfill their potential and reflect the glory of Christ.